I rea[illegible] meeting you! Stay in touch!

4 WEEKS TO YOUR AMERICAN DREAM JOB

The simple path to getting a visa, learning cultures and leading the life you want

Michael Patrick Miller

Published in the United States by Culture Adapt Publishing.

Library of Congress Cataloging-in-Publication Data
Miller, Michael.

4 Weeks To Your American Dream Job: The simple path to getting a U.S. visa, learning cultures and leading the life you want / Michael Patrick Miller

Includes bibliographical references.
1. Quality of work life. 2. Self-employment. 3. Self-transformation. 4. Quality of life. 5. Career success. I. Title. II. Title: Four Weeks To Your American Dream Job. III. Title: The simply path to getting a U.S. visa, learning cultures and leading the life you want.

ISBN: 978-0-9890768-1-4

First Edition

For Asie

Your strength and support allowed me to complete one of my dreams. I'm forever in debt to your kindness and so lucky to have you in my life.

Contents

Get Articles, Recommendations, Tips and Invitations To Free Classes Join My Private Email List

If you want to get invitations to free classes, articles, recommendations and tips, send an email to privatelist@cultureadapt.com, with "private list" in the subject heading. I'll also email you, as a thank-you for purchasing this book, these three free digital downloads related to my book:

- Bonus interview with serial-entrepreneur Amarpreet Sawhney. As you'll read this book you'll hear about his amazing journey from India to Texas, from PhD to companies generating billions of dollars. In this exclusive video recording, he gives his tips and tricks to life, entrepreneurship and success.

- Career Blueprint & Self Assessment tools. These two tools are incredibly important to your success and discussed in length later in the book.

- A Learning and Resources guide with links to all resources mentioned in this book, for further study and implementation.

I send only quality content I've written myself to my e-mail list, no spam, and I never give your information to anyone else. You can remove yourself at any time with one click.

Once again, to get immediate access to everything described above for free, just send an e-mail to privatelist@cultureadapt.com with "private list" in the subject header.

FAQ - Doubters read this

Is this book for you? Chances are that it is. Here are some of the most common questions, doubts and fears that people encounter before taking action and getting a job in the United States:

Do I have to be an international student in America?
No. I realize that everyone's situation is different. What if you're currently outside the country? Maybe you're looking for a job in a small specific industry? Perhaps you're an executive looking to make the move to America, or have interviews scheduled but are not sure how to "ace" them.

Regardless of your specific background, this book is packed with proven strategies and templates for every possible situation. It gives you everything you need to meet more important people, get more interviews, and get more job offers.

What if I'm looking for an internship or co-op instead of a full-time job?
The strategies I teach in this book are necessary to get internships as well as full-time positions. Throughout the book I list various resources that are valuable to an internship job search.

What if I have a job already... but I don't like it?
This book will help you get the job you've always dreamed about. It will teach you how to follow your passions and find something you really love.

Is an H-1B visa the only immigration option?
No. There are many other visas available and I'll discuss all of them and which you may be eligible for.

Do I need to be an Ivy League graduate?
Nope. Most of the success stories in this book didn't attend the world's most elite universities— some didn't even graduate college. The simple reality is that certain colleges have better corporate connections than others, but this does not *determine* success. The people that use the strategies in this book will have a leg up on all of their competition, Ivy League or otherwise.

So why can't I learn this somewhere else?
In my experience with career coaches, recruiters and professional companies, I have discovered that they don't have the *time* to design a program **specifically tailored** to international individuals.

I've spent months tirelessly working to design this system. I worked directly with international individuals and combined my knowledge of visa laws and cultural differences to craft a unique global approach. Of course, I combined this with my own business experience in a management position at a **Fortune 500 company** (attained only three years after my graduation from university, and without the expected ten year's of experience).

What if my English isn't great, or I'm not great at networking?
No problem. I'll teach you how to network, build relationships quickly and even some tricks to learn English faster.

I truly believe the material I cover in this book can help anyone succeed, with much less frustration along the way. Some people thrive in an environment of networking, connecting to people, interviewing and talking to hundreds of different companies. But some of us find this approach to obtaining a job stressful and intimidating.

This could be due to a bad experience, or just personal preference. Whatever the situation, this book gives you simple strategies that allow you to overcome those anxieties and get a job offer—even if a company has told you "we don't sponsor visas."

What if I'm an American? Is the book still useful?

Yes. Just skip Chapter 2 on immigration law and follow the rest of the strategies in the book.

My Story and Why You Need This Book

"Don't Let The Fear of Striking Out Keep You From Playing The Game." - *Babe Ruth*

I grew up in one of the least-diverse places in America: Lyndonville, Vermont (a.k.a. "The Northeast Kingdom"). Population: 5,900. Diversity? Non-existent: the town is 96.82% white. The roads are mostly dirt, snow falls in feet (not inches), the internet is delivered via dial-up (that is, through phone lines) and just about everyone has a truck with a shotgun in the back window. But wait…before you assume that I am a close-minded American and declare that I couldn't know a thing about life of an international student, you should know that I'm the Founder of Culture Adapt, a company that's changing the way people develop their global careers.

I will admit that it is a strange profession for someone of my origins. My perspective, though, is shaped by where I have come from. So, without divulging too much information too quickly, let me first tell you about my journey and how I came to write this book.

It was 2003, and I was about to start freshman year at Worcester Polytechnic Institute. I had managed to make my escape from my small, country town, with hopes of becoming something more than a logger.

I was excited for the new adventure that college represented: new friends, a new city, a new culture…in a sense, a new life. It would be a constant learning experience.

I had received an e-mail stating that my freshman roommate would be Ivan LaBruna, from Italy. I had never met an Italian person before, and was eager to get to know him. In fact, it didn't even occur to me to question his language skills or accent; I simply wanted to meet someone new, with an unusual background and different view on life. Within the first week I could tell Ivan would be a life-long friend of mine. Because we got along so well, I was often invited to International Student Council events with him. I found myself speaking to students from India, Cyprus, Venezuela, Costa Rica and China…for this redneck kid from the middle-of-nowhere, Vermont, it was truly an eye-opening experience.

Eventually, I became a steady member of the group, attending so many get-togethers that I was soon referred to as "The American." Why? Because I was the *only* American among them. At the time, Americans weren't encouraged to participate in international events. Not discouraged, but not *en*couraged, either. So why was I able to "infiltrate" this group of international students? Was it my knowledge of cross-culturalism? Was it the fact that I'd been around the world and was culturally competent? No, simply that I was open-minded and interested to learn.

Later, I joined another social group on campus: a fraternity (in its own way a cultural club). I was happy to have been accepted into two different groups, but noticed immediately a barrier between my international and fraternity friends. There seemed to be lack of understanding, an inability to communicate. And the issue did not stem from one side alone: both the American fraternity guys *and* the diverse internationals contributed to this friction.

From my sophomore year to my senior year, I had two lives; one with the fraternity brothers and one with my international friends. As time went on I noticed that something similar was happening with the different ethnic social groups that comprised the international student body. Chinese hung out with Chinese. Latinos hung out with Latinos. Turkish students with fellow Turks, and so on. I found myself connected to each group, but ultimately, a member of none. I lamented the loss of cohesion in our global group, and began to consider *why* students began to isolate themselves.

However, this particular experience didn't prove true was when I lived abroad in Hong Kong my junior year. I was there with a multicultural group of students from WPI and for most of the American students, it was our first times living outside the country. We found ourselves in a similar situation: in a vastly different culture, with a different language and a constant flow of new experiences. Everyone had to keep an open mind to enjoy their time there and become successful. This similar mindset helped our entire group build relationships with one another and people that weren't friends at WPI, became best friends.

When my time in Hong Kong finished, I returned to WPI with a new mindset, knowing that I had grown as a person. I hoped to bring these new views to the two groups of people in my life.

At first, it seemed as though it was going to work, but sadly, I failed to bring the two groups of people together. Without them both having the commonality of being in a new culture, it seemed that they didn't feel the need to coexist.

As college came to an end I continued to ponder this situation and knew I needed to experience more of the world. With a degree was in Chemical Engineering and a passion for new cultures, I became extremely focused on getting into a rotational development program as a Process Engineer—particularly one that would give me international experience.

Luckily, numerous programs offered this type of arrangement. I interviewed older fraternity brothers that had entered these development programs, met company representatives at career fairs and constantly looked online for other opportunities. Eventually, after many applications and interviews, I was presented with a job offer at Hollingsworth & Vose.

As a result, in 2007 I began my professional career in their leadership development program. During that two-year program, I was sent to five different manufacturing facilities, including one in Suzhou, China. It was during my stay in China that I found myself blankly staring at my office wall. I had only been living there for a couple of months but was feeling extremely depressed and homesick. In all my travels to fifteen-plus foreign countries, I had never experienced such a sensation. I felt alone, out of place, and less intelligent. I had always prided myself on my openness to new cultures and ability to connect with people from different parts of the world, yet here I sat, heart-sick and unable to even admit to anyone that I was having a problem.

Unfortunately, I never sought out help and continued to feel depressed for the rest of my stay in Suzhou. My work performance suffered and I was not able to make many new friends. I counted the days until I was able to get on a plane back to Boston.

It is worth noting that my failure was not just personal: I had failed to adapt to the business world, too.

When the rotational development program was at an end, I found that I wasn't promoted as quickly as I had hoped. Desirous to find greater prospects, I started looking for another job. I wasn't just looking for any job though: I was looking for a challenge. I found a target in Dean Foods, a Fortune 500 company whose available position for Continuous Improvement Manager (change management) demanded ten years of experience.

I want to highlight the significance of this choice. If I had listened to the job posting, the first person who interviewed me or my peers, I would have never even applied to that position—and I never would have secured it. Instead, I overcame the fear of possible rejection and failure. This skill is something I worked hard to master, and will be teaching you later in the book.

My time at Dean foods was very successful. I was able to save the company a few million dollars in costs, while acting as the youngest manager in my facilities by about 15 years. Though I was challenged by the experience, I still felt that I could do more.

At this point, I made the decision to start my event marketing company, Socialete. It was exhilarating to be my own boss and finally be in charge of my own destiny. One of the best parts of the experience was my ability to employ three international students.

They were all amazingly smart, likable and dedicated employees. However, as graduation neared they started voicing their concern about getting a job and being able to stay in America. Through my employees, I began to learn more of the many barriers facing international students, including language skills, networking ability and visa issues.

In addition to these obstacles, I noticed as their employer many cultural barriers: from e-mail writing to conversation techniques. I realized that the greatest stumbling block impeding their success in America was this foreign *business* culture—the very stumbling block that had prevented my being successful in China.

As graduation day approached, the international students became more worried about their prospects. The small defeats were not confidence-boosting, either: companies did not return calls, hiring managers declared that they did not sponsor visas, etc. I continued to hear things like,

"I don't think there's any companies that sponsor visas."

"I heard there's no visas left to give out."

"I think I'll probably go back to my home country to find a job."

While it is true that some companies will not call back, and many may not hire, I realized that these limiting thoughts were the ones preventing my employees from ultimately holding their dream job.

Since my trip to Hong Kong, I have lived in Suzhou, China and traveled to over thirty countries. I have founded two companies and employed people from eight different countries. Throughout these experiences, I have observed one commonality: *there is a lack of business culture education everywhere in the world.* Not just at universities, but in offices, neighborhoods, and clubs.

In 2011, University of Hartford professor Abrahao Araujo declared that the "perceived support from interpersonal networks in the host country and from online ethnic social groups was negatively related to social difficulties." In layman's terms: ethnic social groups have an isolating impact, stunting social exploration. With evidence gathered from personal experience (such as my time at WPI), I can confidently agree. The audacity, initiative and energy I see in international student community are unmatched. Yet I fear that by clinging to the comfort of isolated social groups, these individuals hinder their own experience, and the experience of other Americans like myself. Only when people from different nations can extend their influence beyond their cultural comfort zone will we begin to understand each other, personally and professionally.

As a result of my own personal experience at university and in the workplace, I find myself able to assist thousands of international individuals in their pursuit of the American lifestyle and profession of their choice. Now, I am able to offer this book, as well, with the hope that it will provide the intercultural communication and job-getting skills to allow you to be successful.

With this book, you will learn that a passionate, fast-acting, hard-working, bold and confident individual can achieve his or her ideal profession.

I know what you're thinking: "Oh, sure: I can get my dream job just with passion. Really, Mike?"

Yes! Absolutely!

That's how I started Culture Adapt, my past company, and secured the different job positions that I have held. I've done it all on passion, and I guarantee you that will carry you further in life than anything else.

Right now, I want you to promise to yourself that you're going to take action WHILE you read this book. With each day and each chapter, you come one step closer to getting your dream job! If you don't find yourself exactly where you hope to be in the next four weeks, then promise yourself to continue the pursuit of your dream. Don't give up!

Time to begin. I want you to get out a pen and paper and write down what your goal is in BIG letters. Have a look at a few examples:

Do you want to get your first interview in 4 weeks?

Do you want to get multiple interviews?

Do you want to get a job offer in 4 weeks?

Do you want to get multiple job offers and then negotiate for a higher price?

Sounds overwhelming, right?

Remember: you can do it. With your goal in mind on every step of your journey, and my help through this book, you can achieve it.

I ask you, regardless of your background, to go beyond your comfort zone and see where it takes you.

Chronology of a Career Optimist

This book will teach you the precise principles I have used to:

- Become a manager of two facilities at a Fortune 500 company
- Get a six-figure salary at age 25
- Successfully implement business program in China
- Earn a chemical engineering degree with minimal effort
- Save companies over three million dollars while employed there
- Negotiate a $10,000 salary increase
- Become a professional lecturer at top universities
- Start two companies
- Become an employer of people from eight different countries
- Travel to over 30 countries
- Teach over 500 international individuals how to communicate more effectively

Where it began:

December 22, 1984 Born with a twin sister, Natalie. We have been competing ever since. She now has her own successful comedy study company, SparkArts, located in Burlington, Vermont.

1994 My fourth grade teacher, Mrs. Gorham, pulls me out of the classroom by my ear because I was being such a brat. Still one of the most memorable moments of my early school career. Sometimes we are not mature enough to understand our mentors.

1998 Start my first job as a brick mason's assistant after crashing a friend's dad's snowmobile into a telephone pole the previous winter. It was a valuable life lesson and I learned how to work hard.

2001 Leave the United States for the first time, to visit an exchange student friend, Jannis Pulm, in Germany. I get an extremely bad ear ache on the plane ride over and have my first experience in a foreign hospital. Among the more pleasant memories include my first taste of beer, and some amazing sites. I also went to Amsterdam…just to see the sites.

2002 I have my first major life failure in my final year of high school basketball. My team went 8-13 and didn't make it past the first round of playoffs. I had dedicated well over 10,000 hours to this sport and it crushed me.

2003 Graduate high school from Lyndon Institute and start my college career at Worcester Polytechnic Institute.

Fall 2003 Meet my Italian roommate, Ivan LaBruna, and join the international student council. I meet amazing people from all over the world.

2006 Study abroad in Hong Kong. This is truly an eye-opening experience and one of the best times of my life. It is during this time that I decide I want to have a global career.

2007 Meet one of the most influential people in my life, Sharon Wulf, in her Organizational Behavior & Science class. This is the first college class I actually enjoy, and I find a mentor in Professor Wulf, as she believes in me before I believed in myself.

2007 Get my first job in a rotational leadership development program at Hollingsworth & Vose. It is precisely the job I had wanted and know it will accelerate my career.

2008 Move to Kathleen, Georgia, where I don't know a single person in the state. During this time, I completely change as a person and grow more than at any other time in my life. In addition, I learn about the culture of the "Deep South," and avoid winter for the first time in my life!

Late 2008 Complete my Lean Six Sigma Black Belt certification faster than anyone else ever had in my company, making me an expert in my field.

Winter 2009 Move to Suzhou, China with only two weeks notice and unable to speak or understand a word of Mandarin. At this time, I am not very enthusiastic about the experience. Shortly after arriving, I notice that the culture is vastly different from my own.

Fall 2009 I am diagnosed with narcolepsy. I call my dad to excitedly tell him I was right all along: that all the times I fell asleep in class weren't because I stayed up late, but were in fact my narcolepsy. Knowing that I have this disease helps me to overcome it.

2010 Land a managerial position at Dean Foods, a Fortune 500 company. This is a giant salary and career leap.

2011 Start my first company, Socialete, with no previous entrepreneurial experience. I still somehow manage to win runner-up in the Lean Startup Challenge.

Fall 2011 Acceptance into the Startup Leadership Program continues to build my global network and business expertise.

2012 Employing three international student interns from Hult International Business School prompts me to found my second company, Culture Adapt. It combines my passions of helping others and exploring new cultures.

2012 Become guest lecturer and professional speaker at conferences and universities. Create first online career development course for international individuals trying to get America jobs.

2013 Publish my first book. Something I had previously believed I wouldn't do for another 20 year

Part 1:
Aim Straight

"The Biggest Challenge is In Your Mind" -
Sheila Lirio Marcelo

Chapter 1 - The Choice

"You have to expect things of yourself before you can do them."
Michael Jordan

"Always be yourself, express yourself, have faith in yourself, do not go out and look for a successful personality and duplicate it." *Bruce Lee*

The Road Less Taken

Krishna has sold one company and founded another groundbreaking company, dwinQ. He has achieved some of his dreams and had an extraordinary experience along the way. He grew up in India, a country where expectations for science, technology, engineering and math are set at the highest bar. A place where he feels that there really isn't a huge focus on communication skills; where people are taught if they get their math right, their science right, then something else will fall into place.

Yet Krishna learned from his father that this is not true. Instead, he was taught that you need a wholesome upbringing, a wholesome quality in yourself. As a result, he never underestimated the value of communication. It was difficult to reconcile this respect for communication skills with his own background, though. Krishna came from a very modest background: a low-to-middle class family. His father was paid enough to provide the necessities, but not to fund a dream. At times, not even enough to feel secure or provide any guarantees of success. In India, the only thing that can help you transform your own lifestyle is education and knowledge. These "life-jackets" may keep you afloat, and eventually help you swim to a more comfortable lifestyle.

His father knew this and always pushed him to succeed academically. Eventually, Krishna became fluent in English.

However, no sense of entrepreneurship was ever instilled. His father had been a full-time employee at the same company for 40 years. He had no idea what entrepreneurship was or how it should be done. Without adult guidance, Krishna's journey to entrepreneurial success was not a fast one. Despite the hindrances he faced, Krishna's dream began like that of many immigrant's: to come to America, work for a large corporation and live his dream life.

In the second year of his undergraduate studies in India, he knew that coming to America would be essential to his career and life goals. At the time, there were no big technology companies in India—no outsourcing or I.T. boom. Thus, the decision seemed black-and-white: there was little for him in India, while America overflowed with the wealth of all the different technology companies. So he moved to the U.S., beginning his M.A. and Ph.D. at Texas A&M University. He was successful in his studies, and managed to secure his dream job after graduation in 1996. His new position? Principal Architect for one of the largest and most respected technology companies in the world, Digital Equipment Corporation (DEC). Krishna had a finally achieved his dream. His job in America was one that many lower-to-middle class children from India aspired to.

For the next four years, he worked at DEC. He found exciting work to do, and felt at ease in a work environment that looked beyond differences in culture, language, and ethnic backgrounds. For that reason, Krishna states that he loves America. "If you are contributing, if you're making a difference for the company," he adds, "it doesn't matter where you're from."

Despite all of the excitement and positivity at DEC, something strange happened. This dream that he had since childhood started to fade. His enthusiasm for the work decreased, and soon he realized that it was not enough. It was no longer his dream.

He had originally chosen to work in traditional research at DEC because he thought that he could apply his research to their products. This was not the case. The output of his work at DEC mattered to him personally, but it didn't make any difference to the company, nor did it have a macro impact on the world. Eventually he decided, "Fine: this was a start but this is not what I want to continue. I need to be in a faster-paced environment where the output matters." In his mind he had made a calculation, one that involved his sacrifice to leave his own country, family and friends. One that included the satisfaction an engineer gets from creating something amazing. One that included all the risks he had been willing to take. A calculation that helped him realize that if he was going to stay in America, he better do something that makes a difference on both a micro and macro level.

On the micro level, it would be leading a team and making a difference to the people that work for him. Trying to make them appreciate the successes and learn from their failures. On the macro level, he wanted to develop technologies that really matter and have a positive impact on the world. He wanted to create something that would be used by millions of people. These two desires drove him to start working for startups and eventually start his own company.
So why couldn't he do that at DEC?

He knew that there were executives in the company who could quickly make a difference at a macro level, as their status gave them much more opportunities to do so. He also knew that many of them were not creating the change, just driving it. It was his personal dream to create.

While working at one of the pioneers in the Internet era, Krishna had learned the communication and cooperative skills and norms necessary to succeed in American business. He had followed a career path that helped him get a green card, thereby giving him more mobility and chance to do something on his own.

At last, he took a chance, by beginning to work with start-ups and eventually founding his own. He would later sell this first company, only to start yet another company. Why this continuous shifting and changing? Krishna explains his view of himself as being "naked." He does not have layers of funding, layers of management, or layers of employees to heal himself. He is responsible for his company and if he screws up, the entire company is affected. However, if the company succeeds, it makes a difference to both his team and the world. The constant movement from one project to another allows for this personal accountability. And of course, Krishna pursues the challenge. As one personal mentor told him,

"It's easy to do things wrong, and very difficult to do things right."

Krishna tries to do the difficult things—and do them to the best of his ability.

Your Social Transformation

This is your life.

"Your" is the key word in that sentence. I want you to remember that forever. Your career can go anywhere and you can be anything, and throughout this, the only opinion you should care about is your own. Many parents dream of their children's success from birth. They think their son or daughter will be a great doctor, lawyer, engineer, executive, entrepreneur, or take over the family business. They try to mold them to fit that dream.

While I truly believe that all parents want what is best for their children, their vision of your life is not the one that matters. Too often, people follow that path set by their parents and end up unhappy, shrouded in regret. This is why you must live for yourself. As Krishna's life-story shows us, the socially ascribed status of your parents does not determine the rest of your life. Only you determine that.

The things you are born into do not define you as a person and definitely do not shape the rest of your life. The actions you take to earn new abilities, merits, and skills will define you.
Many of the people I mention in this book (including myself), don't come from wealth, instead creating it on their own. Others have come from wealth and have chosen to earn it on their own. These people come from different races, genders, education and family backgrounds. Everyone has their own unique success story with many obstacles along the way, but all found the strength to overcome.

You now must find yours.

Wei's Path

Wei was comfortable in his Beijing home, surrounded by friends and family. He was happy, enjoying life and the culture that he was a part of. Despite this, his parents dreamed that he would one day leave Beijing and move to America. This had always been their dream and they had never quite accomplished it.

That day finally came after Wei completed his Bachelor's Degree in Chemistry. His parents had decided that it was best for him to go to graduate school in America. They pushed him to apply, he did and eventually was accepted to Rensselaer Polytechnic Institute (RPI), an impressive engineering school. He still had no desire to move to the States but finally decided to go, at the constant insistence of his parents.

Despite having made the decision largely at the behest of his parents, Wei chose to apply for financial aid and pay for college himself so he could be on his own instead of relying financially on his parents. This was start of his transformation.

Located about three hours north of New York City in the city of Troy, New York, RPI felt a world away from Beijing. Troy's population of 800,000 made it feel like a village in comparison to Wei's home-city of 20 million people. It was hard to adapt to

American culture in the beginning, especially because he didn't speak English well. His classes were hard and studying kept him busy most of his days, so much so that he barely had time to socialize. He began to feel isolated and unhappy with the choice he had made.

The only thing that kept him going was his desire to be independent. He ventured onward, finishing his degree program at RPI and getting a job in a big pharmaceutical company. He had finally achieved the dream his parents had set for him but something was missing, he was still unhappy.

He decided that it was time to move on to another company and continue pursuing his own dreams. He tried to find meaning at different companies, moving from New York, to Connecticut, to Seattle, to New Jersey, then Boston. At any point he could have moved back home, his parents even asked him to return to Beijing, but he refused to give up. In the end, his parents were right to convince him to move to America, but when he did, he started following his own difficult path.

As time went by, Wei became more outgoing. He began befriending more Americans and familiarizing himself with the language and culture. This built his confidence and allowed him to feel more at home. He understood that many Chinese people come to America and take an easier path. He knew it would be easy for him to only hang out with Chinese, watch Chinese shows online, eat at Chinese restaurants, read the news in Chinese…in short, to continue a Chine lifestyle in the United States.

Yet Wei knew that to truly succeed, he'd have to be different. He'd have to immerse himself. He realized that ultimately, attempts to recreate far-away home-communities could be more of a limitation than a positive boost. He believes "we are all the same, we are all people. We may speak different languages and be from different places but we are still the same." Bearing this in mind, Wei continued to move forward in America.

Like Krishna, Wei now has a green card and ability to do whatever he chooses in America. His true passion it is writing, not chemistry, and he one day he dreams of being a published author. While he is not going to quit his current job to pursue this dream, he has provided himself with an environment where he can easily do both.

As proof, here is his first piece of published writing:

"My dad has been a high school administrator all his life. Growing up, I also remember that he liked to bring a camera and take pictures wherever we went. However, only until recently did I find out that becoming a photographer has been a dream of his since he was a teenager.

Thirteen years ago, after graduating from college in Beijing, I came to the U.S. by myself. My life was busy with school and then work. I hardly had any time for hobbies. Only when I drifted further and further away from my own dreams, had I realized how difficult it was for my dad to keep his alive for over 40 years.

My dad retired seven years ago, and he finally had time to do the things he likes. Recently, he emailed me some photos he took and I was so impressed by them. Then an idea formed: why not have an exhibition at my office building, the Cambridge Innovation Center, for my dad to fulfill his dream?

I showed the photos to a building manager, Monika. I am very grateful that not only did she agree to display the photos, she hand-picked the photos with me and her "uptown" team, including Joel and Sarah. They even helped me set up the whole exhibition. I invite everyone to come to my dad's small photo exhibition in Cambridge, Massachusetts. I hope you will enjoy them. If you do, please also remember that my dad, a 67-year-old retiree in Beijing, is a living proof that it is never too late to pursue your dreams." - Wei

My Path

My parents were so proud of me when I got into WPI. They were proud of me when I graduated, when I got my first job and when I got a really great job at a Fortune 500 company.

"You are on the fast track to being really successful, Michael," they would often tell me. They were always happy to see me progress towards their vision of my future success, in which I would someday sit as the rich Vice President or CEO of a giant corporation. The only problem with this future was that this was not my dream.

I had thought it was for a while. Growing up in a normal middle-class family in Vermont had inspired in me a desire to be extravagantly wealthy (how I achieved this goal seemed, at the time, less important). All I cared about was the end result: being able to travel wherever I want, buy whatever I want and do whatever I want.

So I got a chemical engineering degree, because it was the highest paid starting salary for a college graduate. Unfortunately, I never liked it nor even found it interesting. The one class I did enjoy in college was Organizational Behavior & Science, taught by my mentor Sharon Wulf. Yet I didn't heed the warning signs. Instead, I assumed that I would really enjoy the career-version of my chemical engineering degree—that this would somehow differ from what I had seen at school.

I was wrong. Just three months after starting my first job, I began to dislike going into work. My initial ecstatic feeling had worn off and I wondered if the money I was making was worth it. Eventually I decided the money was worth it, and that to be satisfied I just had to make more. So with the hope that it would lead to bigger and better paychecks, I continued my work at this first job.

I was financially comfortable, with the means to do pretty much anything I wanted. This did allow me to really enjoy my time outside of work, but this comforting fact faded when I came to the abrupt realization that sixty percent of my waking hours were spent at work. Sixty percent of my life spent doing something I didn't care about.

I decided I needed a change. I started reading books on entrepreneurship and business, thinking it was time to start my own company. I educated myself on many things that I had never learned in school and were interesting to me. I started to notice that my network of friends and business connections weren't aligned with this new interest.

At the time, I didn't understand this network paradox that I was in. I didn't understand that staying inside this network would continue fuel the dream that had been given to me in childhood. And before I knew it, I had forgotten entrepreneurship and decided that I needed to get a job making even more money. I did just that. It was more focused on things I enjoyed, like innovation and training others, but still was not in a field that I cared about. Still, for some reason I thought this job would make me happy.

I was wrong. Again, just three months after starting, I had grown tired of the job and the nice salary increase had completely lost it's effect. I realized that I was stuck in the same situation that I was in a few years earlier. My success, money and progress had not made me happy. This is when I knew I needed to re-evaluate my dream. Was I following my own, or the one set by my parents? Is money what I really wanted? Or was it freedom? Was it being a CEO of Fortune 500 company? Or being the founder of my own, doing something I loved and helping others around me?

After this self-reflection, I was able to break out of my network paradox, got the right mentors and started my first company without fear. I have never regretted this choice I made years ago. Giving up the cushy job, the salary, the corporate trips and trainings. I am doing what I want and living my own life. My parents still do not completely understand my choice but they have never stopped supporting me. They respect what I have done and understand that it is not their dream that I must follow.

I remember I used to blame them and others for the years it took me to start following my own dream. I used to think, "If only my parents had taught me about entrepreneurship at a younger age." "If only I had not gone to college for Chemical Engineering and racked up all this student loan debt." "If only I had grown up in a city, instead of a town, I would have got here faster..."

I don't have those thoughts anymore. I realize that where I am from, what I have done and how I have been taught throughout my life is all part of my own unique journey. All my experiences have been invaluable and while I have changed my career path, I remain the same person at my core. The same values, the same things I enjoy and the same drive that will one day lead me to achieve all my dreams.

The same person my parents had always dreamed of raising.

Your Turning Point

Throughout your life there will be many times where you have a choice. Two paths, dramatically different in how they will shape you as a person. These paths are often difficult to recognize, and if you are not concentrated on a lifelong goal you will choose incorrectly—even by accident.

Many don't understand the individual nature of Americans, which can allow people to live their lives based on their own desires and expectations for themselves. Still, I believe that even those who come from very different backgrounds can achieve this same sense of individualism.

Being an individual employee, entrepreneur, student or specialist does not mean playing exclusively by your own rules, though. At times, you must also be willing to change yourself to fit the part. You must present yourself in a way that will impress your target audience. Sometimes this means changing your accent or speech patterns (I have done this), changing your dress (I have done this), or changing your appearance (I have done this) to fit your desired social identity. You also need to be ready to distance yourself from those that are inconsistent with this identity.

Now, understanding that you must accept a difficult path and embracing the personal changes that path may require, you can make it happen. If your dream is to become a CEO of Fortune 100 company, plan out how you are going to get there. If your dream is to start an American company like Krishna, think about the path you have to follow. If you can't stand the thought of ever working for someone else and need to start your own company before you get a visa, you need to find investors. If your dream is to live in America, make it happen.

Always remember, too, that getting a job is just a stepping stone for your career. It is only beginning of your journey to happiness and success in your career, and your entire life. Life is short, but if you are focused on what YOU really want to accomplishment, you enjoy every minute of it.

Question & Actions

I feel lost and alone. How do I overcome this?
Many of us (myself included) have experienced this feeling. You can overcome any feeling and any situation by believing in yourself. Take a deep breath. Find something proactive to do. Do it. I believe that everyone can accomplish great things if they are willing to work hard.

Why do I need investors if I want to start a company before getting a visa?
Currently, it is not easy for immigrant entrepreneurs to start a company and obtain visas without a large amount of funding. Though there are people working to pass laws to change this, you cannot rely on future changes to make your own choices today. You

have to think about your situation and seize the opportunity. Remember, it took Krishna a little longer than others to start a company but he is doing exactly what he wants now.

I have a job that I'm not really passionate about but it gives me financial security. I'm thinking about doing it for another couple years before I switch jobs. Will waiting really hurt me in any way?
Yes, both mentally and financially. People tend to only meet expectations when they don't love what they do. You can't create anything innovative and amazing if you're not passionate. Subconsciously, you know you don't care and this negatively affects your day-to-day mood. A couple years could change your attitude and approach on the rest of your life.

I want you to sit down and close your eyes. Imagine that your life two years from now if you continue on your same path. What would you feel like? Would you be proud of yourself? Open your eyes, pause, and reflect for a minute. Then close your eyes again and imagine your life two years from now and you are doing something you love and accomplished something amazing! What does that feel like?

Realizing the difference is the start of your journey to happiness and I will be your guide. The lessons in this book will show you what you need to do to follow your own dream and become successful. Just keep reading.

I feel trapped in my current job. I can't switch companies because I'm scared that I will not be able to find another company willing to sponsor my green card. What should I do?
You can actually use this circumstance to your advantage. You already have the security of one job and the freedom to look for another. You should have more confidence because of your current job and there are time constraints. After reading this book you'll know exactly how to get an offer from another company, and once you do, you can try to negotiate for a green card. Imagine if you could

get a company to immediately apply for a green card, instead of waiting the usual six-year period.

Tools & Resources

Startup Leadership Program (www.startupleadership.com)
A highly selective, 80-hour, 6-month world-class training program and lifetime network for outstanding founders and innovators in 20 cities around the world. SLP Fellows have founded 300 companies and raised $200 million. It's great for professionals that have jobs and want to get more involved in startups.

The Innovation Movement (www.declareinnovation.com)
The Consumer Electronics Association (CEA) launched The Innovation Movement to bring together an engaged community not just of industry professionals and entrepreneurs but of all citizens who believe innovation is critical to American global leadership and economic growth. This grassroots campaign mobilizes Americans in support of public policies –such as international trade, skilled immigration, deficit reduction and broadband deployment – that encourage and advance American business and shore up our economy for future generations.

Chapter 2 - Understanding Visa Laws*

"The success I have achieved in bodybuilding, motion pictures, and business would not have been possible without the generosity of the American people and the freedom here to pursue your dreams."
Arnold Schwarzenegger, former Governor of California

Beating the Odds

Mihaela had just lost her first American job after two solid years and was suddenly facing a scary immigration situation. Without an American company sponsoring her work visa, she knew that she needed help. She contacted an immigration attorney immediately to find out her options. He told her the laws describing how long you can legally stay in the country without sponsorship are vague, but sixty days is usually the limit.

Sixty days. That's a lot of pressure, isn't it?

Mihaela had worked hard to find a career she loved and had invested the last seven years building her American career and relationships. Now, in order to stay in America and continue to pursue her passions, she only had one choice: to take action. The lawyer had advised her that she had three options: 1) find a company to sponsor her 2) apply for a visitor's visa to extend her stay for three more months (though this would jeopardizes her immigrant status) 3) apply to school and change to student visa status or 4) get married.

Not ready to hit the books or go down the aisle, she began to look for a company to sponsor her. She didn't sit back and only apply online to jobs, though. Instead, Mihaela used her network and interpersonal skills. She was a Quantative Market Researcher and found twenty companies she would like to work for. The day she lost her job, she sat down and made a plan of action that included:

- Quickly update résumé
- Identity strengths
- Reach out to her network
- Decide on job title
- Identify target companies
- Expand her network
- Reach key decision-makers
- Become an expert in her field

Within the first week, she connected with the right people at some of the companies, but that wasn't enough. She wanted to get interviews at all twenty companies. So she continued to network online and offline to meet the right people. She went to networking events every single night, travelled to different cities to attend industry-related conferences, and had absolutely no fear when approaching people who might be able to help her in her job-search. At these events, she focused all of her energy on finding and talking to CEOs, CFOs, Directors and other decision-makers. Mihaela, understanding that her Bulgarian contacts were of little use in the United States, simply walked up to company CEO and said, "This is what I think you can improve and this is how I think I can improve it."

She maximized her time by reading name tags, approaching conference speakers and speaking to few people her age. She was well-read on industry happenings and able to provide interesting insights that added value to the conversations. She had strong opinions that gave lasting impressions, and made sure to follow up with these decision makers the next day. Ultimately, it is this last quality of fearlessness that is one of the best you can have. The ability to approach and engage with anyone is crucial in the modern business world, particularly when you may not have many on-hand connections (i.e. you now live in a foreign country and do not have the same list of contacts and connections that you might back home). In the end, her confidence, and direct, solution-oriented approach led her to find a job and new visa in **25 days!**

In four weeks, she had only applied to her twenty dream companies and had been internally recommended by decision makers at fifteen! Those fifteen recommendations led to ten interviews and two final job offers.

Mihaela proved herself to be a very solution-oriented person. Her ability to explain specifically what she could do for the potential employer made her stand out. By presenting someone with an example of how your presence in the company would benefit and improve their situation, you have given that person a solution, and shown your own potential value. One must also be proactive, as Mihaela demonstrated during her interviews. Whenever the talk of visas came up, she was not concerned: she had done her own research, spoken with an immigration lawyer and knew the steps necessary to finalize a sponsorship. When the topic arose, she was able to reply,

"I need a visa but don't worry, I can explain to you the process and connect you with my lawyer that can do it easily."

Before the first interviews, these companies had no intention to sponsor a visa, and yet were willing to do so for Mihaela. Her case disproves one of the **biggest myths** espoused by foreign nationals: that some companies don't sponsor visas. Simply not true. Almost any company that wants you on the team can sponsor a visa. You just have to be specialized and able to help that company succeed.

After losing her job, Mihaela could have put her tail between her legs and gone home. She could have got a job in a different country or went to graduate school. Instead, she saw an opportunity to find something better than her previous position, and pursued that chance. During her four-week job search, she discovered a lot about both her career and herself. She never waivered from her passions, her life nor her dreams.

The Expectation

You will not be handed a job. If you think the visa immigration laws are "not fair" and you deserve a job for all your hard work in school, then you might as well stop reading this book right now.

You need to be willing to work **even harder**, overcome your fears, adapt to American business culture and change the way you're approaching your job search. You're literally competing against hundreds of thousands of Americans, international students, foreign nationals, and global business people. You need to act differently to succeed.

B. INTERNATIONAL STUDENT TRENDS

In 2011/12, the number of international students in the U.S. increased 5.7% to a record high of 764,495 students.

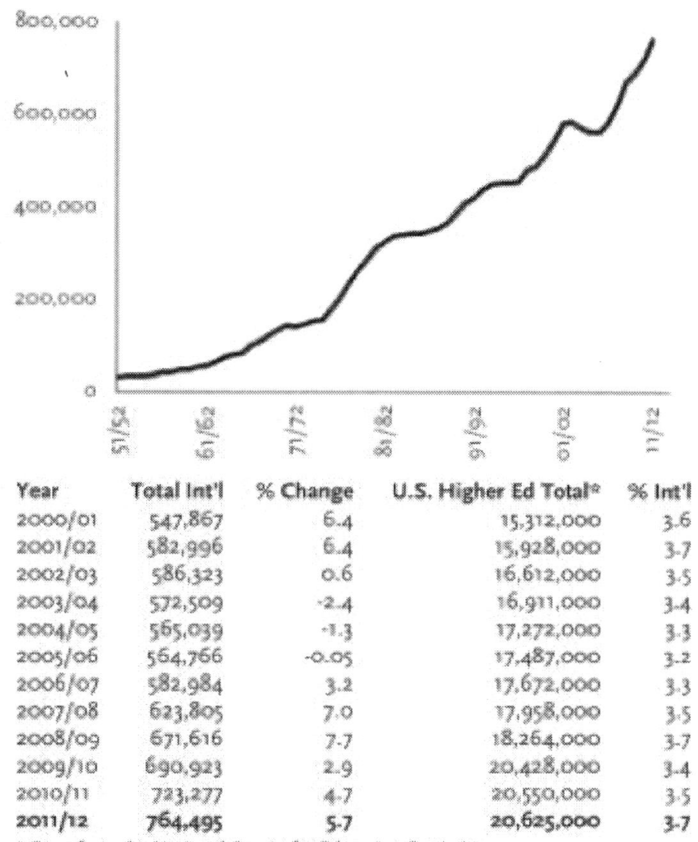

Year	Total Int'l	% Change	U.S. Higher Ed Total*	% Int'l
2000/01	547,867	6.4	15,312,000	3.6
2001/02	582,996	6.4	15,928,000	3.7
2002/03	586,323	0.6	16,612,000	3.5
2003/04	572,509	-2.4	16,911,000	3.4
2004/05	565,039	-1.3	17,272,000	3.3
2005/06	564,766	-0.05	17,487,000	3.2
2006/07	582,984	3.2	17,672,000	3.3
2007/08	623,805	7.0	17,958,000	3.5
2008/09	671,616	7.7	18,264,000	3.7
2009/10	690,923	2.9	20,428,000	3.4
2010/11	723,277	4.7	20,550,000	3.5
2011/12	**764,495**	**5.7**	**20,625,000**	**3.7**

* Data from the National Center for Education Statistics

As you can see from this chart [1], the U.S. international student population is steeply increasing year after year. It is projected to top 800,000 students this year and will only continue growing.

The problem is that the number of H-1B visas (the most sought-after) being issued by the U.S. government *isn't* growing. There is an annual visa "cap" which means that the U.S. government can only issue a certain amount of these visas every year. Currently, the H-1B cap is set at 65, 000 with an extra 20,000 on top of that for people that have master degrees or higher (MBA candidates, PhDs, etc.).

800,000 vs. 85,000. You do the math (and that's only the U.S. international student population—the job market is flooded with global candidates, recent graduates and other American citizens as well).

So how could you possibly get your dream job and visa with those odds?

Don't Believe Everything You Hear

I often tell people that throughout their life they will encounter two choices of travel. One route is easier and less-frightening. The other is road and the other is grueling and time-consuming. Ninety-five percent of people follow road number one. Why?

Because most people are terrified of the unknown. They're worried about getting their feelings hurt, getting rejected, encountering difficult circumstances and failing.

This will not be you. With my guidance, you're going take the road less traveled and come out on top just like Mihaela did.

The first thing I need you to understand is the greatest myth about immigration law: "My dream company said they don't sponsor visas."

The simple truth is that *any* company can sponsor a visa. Absolutely any company.

WOAH!

Did I just blow you mind? I was even shocked when I first learned this.

If you can prove to a company that you will provide enough value to merit sponsoring, they will sponsor you. Yes, this is a difficult task, but if you follow my system you can achieve the results you desire.

More Options Than You Think

There are many different visa options available to foreign nationals. In this section, I will briefly cover each of them so you know what possibilities exist. Often internationals think that the H-1B is the *only* option for employment in the U.S. As a result, they miss out on a viable alternatives like the J-1, O-1, E-3, H-1B1, and the L1 visas.

If you're a student, make sure you consult with the international student office in your school about CPT, OPT or STEM OPT, as this documentation is necessary for everyone who wants to stay in the country.

While I will as comprehensive an overview as possible within the pages of this book, I still strongly suggest you speak with an immigration attorney for "pro bono" advice (provided free of charge) regarding your specific situation. Everyone is from a different country and has different variables involved in their immigration process. The information provided here will allow you to enter the lawyer's office with a confident understanding of your choices, and the ability to make the most of your conversation with the legal professional.

The H-1B

The highly sought-after **H-1B** visa is familiar to most internationals looking to work in the United States. Its popularity stems from the fact that it is the only visa which may lead to eventual permanent resident status. The H-1B allows employers to recruit and hire foreign nationals for a specific period of time (which can be no less than three years and no longer than six years). Typically, an employer will apply for a three-year visa and if the new employee continues to do well, the company may apply again at the end of the second year.

To qualify for an H-1B, you must have a specialty occupation that cannot easily be done by an American. For this reason, it is crucial to be *extremely* specific in your job search (a process which will be discussed in the next chapter). This demand for 'specialization' is intimidating, and many internationals assume that they do not qualify. Bear in mind, though, that your particular job may be done in a broad range of industries and professions. You simply need to be able to correlate your degree and skills to the position of interest.

There are, of course, qualifications for the company, as well. To sponsor you, the employer must have the appropriate credentials and be registered at the state and federal level. They must also be willing to pay you an "equal wage," which means that you must be paid the average wage for your exact title. This is why it's difficult for an immigrant entrepreneur to get a visa.

Once all the qualifications are met, the employer must send your visa application to the U.S. Bureau of Immigration. The approximate cost of this whole process is $1500 – $4000, varying depending on the size of the company (greater or less than 50 employees).

If you visit **myvisajobs.com** you can find a list of all companies that sponsor H-1B visas, sorted by industry, category, etc. Here you will also find additional answers to many questions and laws surrounding the H-1B visa.

Unlimited H-1B's

The U.S. Citizenship and Immigration Services (USCIS) exempts individuals working at certain organizations from the annual H-1B cap. This means that you can work for one of these kinds of companies without having to worry about that 85,000 number.

Specifically, the exemption applies to anyone employed at an institution of higher education; a related or affiliated nonprofit entity; a nonprofit research organization; or a governmental research organization.

Optional Practical Training (OPT)

Optional Practical Training, otherwise known as OPT, can grant temporary employment directly related to an F-1 student's area of study. It is conferred on you once you graduate, and lasts 12 months. You must not leave the country while on it as you may not be able to re-enter America. For the 12-month period, you can work for a company whose work is directly related to your major. This is a great way to show your value to an employer. Remember: when you show yourself to be a valuable employee, a company is much more likely to sponsor you for an H-1B.

Your school will be able to answer any questions you have about applying and getting OPT.

Pre-Completion OPT

This program allows you to work in your field after just one full academic year. The only condition is that the work must be part time. As a result, many international students utilize this visa option for internships. Such internship work experience can be very valuable for undergraduate students, both as a means of gaining situation experience, and an avenue through which you can network and connect to business contacts who may prove very helpful following graduation. Have in mind that any pre-completion OPT will be subtracted from your 12 month OPT limit. So if you have a three month internship, you will only have 9 months left.

Curricular Practical Training (CPT)

CPT allows you to work during your school year. For some degrees, this work experience is mandatory prior to graduation. Northeastern University in Boston, Massachusetts, for example, requires its students to participate in three "co-ops" (internships) before completing their studies. For any work like this, you will need a CPT. The biggest advantage of CPT is that the time will not be subtracted your OPT limit.

STEM OPT (Science, Technology, Engineering, and Mathematics)
This is the same as regular OPT except that it's for science, technology, engineering, and mathematic degrees. If you're wondering if your major falls into one of these categories, you can find out online. STEM OPT candidates can even apply for a 17-month extension.

I should mention that this option can serve as a safety-net when applying for an H-1B. It is possible that an employer's filing does not go through the first year. However, in this case the employer can extend your OPT. This allows you to remain with the company even if the visa cap has already been year that year. The process of application for an H-1B can resume the following year, giving you a great way to stay in the US and keep working for that great company.

J-1
The J-1 is used by a lot of researchers, professors, and short-term visiting scholars. If you're trying to work for university or research firm, you may qualify for this visa. In this situation, the program sponsor must be sponsored by Department of State, rather than a private company. Also, the J-1 visa is distinct in that its recipients must be able to demonstrate non-immigrant intent, and prove residence abroad. In other words, you must have proof a home or apartment ownership in your home country, and need to prove that you have no intent to permanently relocate to America. This is noticeably different from other visa types like the H-1B, which may ultimately lead to U.S. residency. Proving these details of non-immigrant intent can be a little tricky, but an immigration attorney can provide very simple solutions to ensure that you comply with this rule. The ultimate benefit of the J-1 is that it is easy to prepare, faster to obtain and it is also cheaper than the H-1B.

O-1
The O-1, or Extraordinary Ability visa, is a great one to get if you can manage to. Of course, it's difficult to acquire because you must be one

of the top people in your field— in the *world*. Some professions that can receive O-1's include athletes, coaches, musicians, writers, physicists or scientists.

There is no cap for the Extraordinary Ability visa because, frankly, America loves extraordinary people. The only issue with this visa is that in order to remain in America, you must continue to be extraordinary. Essentially, the government has the ability to say that you are no longer extraordinary, and end the visa. The subjective nature of this call has led to many interesting legal situations.

L-1

This visa is for key employees of an international company. To qualify, that company can be located in the U.S. or outside of it, so long as can establish a parent or subsidiary of that company in the US. There's no cap to this visa, either. Consequently, it can be a strong visa option, if you can find an company willing to sponsor it.

An example of such an international company might be World Bank. Let's say you work for World Bank in France, and you decide to get a master's degree in the U.S. If World Bank hires you after graduation, they can easily get you this visa in the States.

Of perhaps you're currently working in a global company and want to move to America. You can go speak to your manager, hiring manager or recruiting manager about the possibility of a foreign stay. They might be able to provide that opportunity through an L-1 visa.

H-1B1

This is the last visa I'll review and is only for citizens of Singapore and Chile. If you're a citizen of either of these countries, you can apply directly at U.S. Consulate abroad. As with the J-1 visa, you must have non-immigrant intent and plan on returning to your home country.

How to find the right immigration attorney

Now that you have a basic understanding of some of the visas available, you should speak to an immigration attorney. Finding the right attorney is crucial to your success, because their counsel will provide you with the most effective, secure means of legally residing in the United States. Keep in mind that some companies will have their own attorneys, but I still strongly advise that you have your own legal contact.

A piece of advice I give my students is that the immigration attorney you choose should be willing to consult you for free. You should feel like you can trust them completely. You should know that they have your best interests in mind and want to help you succeed. If they are not willing to consult you for free, they may not give you the attention you deserve. Of course, there are legal services which you will need to pay for, but basic question-and-answer sessions should be available to you.

To find a lawyer, simply search Google or LinkedIn to search for "immigration attorney" in your city. There will be many options and it's up to you to set up phone calls and meetings with them.

Questions & Actions

What if I speak to a company and they say "We don't sponsor visas."

Earlier in this chapter, I described Mihaela's experience. After losing her job, and with only 60 days to find a new one, she began searching. She really worked her tail off, found 20 target companies, met the right people, got interviews and negotiated a job offer. She never gave them a chance to say this.

She discussed sponsorship once the company was interested in giving her a job. I suggest you try to do the same. Again, you just have to prove your value to the company. At this point the cost of a visa is $1500 - $4000, which is nothing to most companies. Once you have established yourself as a valuable employee whom they are eager to hire, the negotiations of visa paperwork simply become part of the process.

How important is it that I know these laws?

99% of people out there, *especially* Americans, don't understand visa laws. It's a complex and scary thought to some employers. Many don't even know the actual cost of sponsoring a visa. For this reason, you are at a great advantage when you are able to present your future employer with their options. The preparedness on your part will only affirm in your employer's mind your suitability for the job.

Imagine saying to a future employer: "Applying for an H-1B is easy and I have a great chance of being approved because my background matches the exact requirements of this position. The cost is only about $3000, but I think that I could generate that value for you in a week. I have my own immigration attorney ready to file the paperwork for you too."

Instead of, "You can give me a visa, right?"

How do I prepare for the visa discussion with a future employer?

To prepare for this you should write down questions that they may ask you and the appropriate answers. You can do online research, ask people in informational interviews and ask other foreign nationals to come up with these questions.

If I'm outside of the country do I have to tell the companies I'm applying to?

I tell my students that they should have their correct address on their resume but if you are flexible you can find other options. I know of a case where a German businessman was able to fly to America immediately for any interview. In another case, a person was utilizing the 3-month visitors visa. If you have this flexibility, you should make it clear.

Can I pay for my own visa?
No. The employer must pay. You can however pay to expedite the process and decision. If you pay $2000 you will typically get an answer in a couple weeks instead of months.

How do I know whether my job is a "specialty occupation"?
While some occupations are clearly "specialty occupations" as defined by laws and regulations, others are not so clear and the USCIS will make a decision on a case-by-case basis. For some professions such as computer programmer, general manager, librarian, consultant, designer, etc., determination of "specialty occupation" is a complicated process, and many factors will be considered.

What if the visa cap has already been hit?
Still have your company apply. It may get you an extension and allow you to stay in the country for another year, at which point your company can apply again.

When can the H-1B cap petitions be filed?
The past few years have shown that it is best to file H-1B cap cases on April 1st. The USCIS permits H-1B cases to be filed by more than one potential employer on behalf of a single foreign national. However, it is not permissible to have a single employer file multiple H-1B petitions for the same beneficiary in an effort to increase one's chances in the lottery.

Personal Challenge

Ask For Pro-Bono Advice (1 Day)

Call a immigration attorney and ask for pro-bono advice on your specific situation. **Call** is the key word in that sentence. If the first lawyer you ask says "no," call another one. Keep calling until you are successful. If you are overseas, use one of the inexpensive calling services listed below.

Tools & Tricks

Jeff Goldman Immigration (www.jeffoldmanimmigration.com) - A firm that I personally trust and have worked with. Jeff is helpful, respectful and generally a great person to work with. He will analyze your situation and provide accurate advice.

U.S. Citizenship and Immigration Services (www.uscis.gov) - Government-run website that has many free resources, updates and necessary forms.

Viber (www.viber.com) - An app that allows you to make free calls, texts and share pictures with anyone, anywhere. The quality is usually better than Skype.

Skype (www.skype.com) - Make internet calls for free as well as calls and texts from your phone. It's a great tool to use for video interviews.

Google Hangout (www.google.com/+/learnmore/hangouts/) - Chat with any Google user through video calls, host virtual meetings or broadcast globally.

Culture Adapt (www.cultureadapt.com) - Free career advice for international individuals.

*see full disclaimer at back of book

Chapter 3 - Career Blueprint

"Success is the sum of small efforts, repeated day in and day out." - *Robert Collier*

"What do you want?" is too imprecise to produce a meaningful and actionable answer." - *Timothy Ferriss*

Hitting the Bullseye

"Nice to meet you," I said, smiling nervously and as I sat down. My hands were shaking; I hoped the interviewer had noticed when we shook hands.

I was sitting in the small, quiet office of the plant manager at Hollingsworth & Vose. In a moment I would be interviewed for the job of my dreams: a rotational leadership development program that would move me somewhere around the globe every six months, rapidly increasing my expertise and routinely send me to leadership training. I had beat out Ivy-leaguers and students with perfect 4.0 GPA's to get this interview, despite only having a very average 3.0 GPA.

How?

I had very definite goal for myself: to get into a rotational development program, because I knew it would accelerate my career and provide global experience. During my senior year, I had focused 110% of my energy into finding these programs and securing my place in one of them. Honestly, I didn't direct much of my energy towards school. Instead, I pursued these program opportunities relentlessly.

I must have interviewed 20 people that were currently in or had been through one of these programs. I learned exactly what hiring managers were looking for in candidates, exactly what would make someone successful in a program and how they got the job.

I perfected my résumé and cover letter and applied to ten programs that matched my chemical engineering background. I had been asked to interview for five of them and had made it to a final round interview at this particular company.

My nervousness was coupled with excitement, and confidence. I had worked hard to be where I was, and I knew that I could get this job. I proceeded to answer the manager's questions just like I had practiced.

"Yes, I'll be able to work anywhere in world because I really enjoy working with diverse teams. Here is an example..."

"While GPA is important, I find that real world experience and interpersonal skills are more important. For instance, when I worked at..."

"Of course, I've worked with difficult people before but I've always found ways to make them feel like an important part of the team and get them to contribute. There was this one team..."

I was OWNING IT.

Every question he asked I had thought of and knew exactly what I was going to say. I was personable, I showed the right skill set, I was passionate...I knew I was the **perfect fit** for this job.

When the interview ended, he said "Great Mike. Let's take a quick tour around the plant and introduce you to everyone."

I knew this was the final test the company was going to put me through. Would the other employees I was going to be working with like me? Would I fit the company culture?

I was my usual self, smiling, making jokes and being genuinely interested in getting to know these new people. I finished the tour, said my goodbyes and felt pretty good. "That was amazing." I thought to myself.

I had worked so hard to get to this point, been so focused on my goal and finally might have achieved it. It was the kind of feeling of accomplishment that can't be matched. I got in my car and returned home wondering when and if I would get good news.

Sure enough, just two days later I got a phone call from Hollingsworth & Vose.

"Hi Michael, we'd like to offer you the position," the hiring manager said.

"YES! WOOOO! YES! I CAN'T BELIEVE IT!" I thought as I jumped up and down pumping my fists.

"That's great," I said in a calm voice, still fist pumping. "Tell me a little more about the offer."

Goal Setting

You have a goal for the end for this four week period. I want you to write it down and post it on your bathroom mirror, or somewhere else you look every day. That goal should never be forgotten: when you feel discouraged, it will help you overcome the feelings of negativity and self-consciousness.

Of course, having a goal and reaching a goal are two very different things. Where do you even start? Right now, we're going to figure out how you will reach that goal. What is the systematic approach you need to succeed? It's equally important to think about what do you need to do to avoid failure, too.

Don't Be Like Everyone Else

The harsh reality is that the majority of international students and immigrants will find themselves unable to make it past the first interview. Sadly, in that group of dedicated, intelligent international individuals I'm betting there is someone like you. Someone who:

- believed that great grades and a solid resume will get them an interview

- believed that working hard and applying online to 100 jobs will result in an offer

- put in a ton of work, and ***things just didn't work out.***

Naturally, the first question is: "WHY?!!" More importantly, though, we need to ask: how do some people beat the odds, and get a dream job that makes their life complete?

The answer lies in:

The Psychology Behind Why Internationals Fail

Most internationals have HUGE dreams of getting multiple job offers and negotiating them against each other for a big salary. To achieve this great goal, these people are willing to work very hard (sound familiar?).

So what happens?

Eventually, most people give up after a couple months.

Why?

The simple answer is that they have spent TONS of time trying to get a job and have seen NO RESULTS.

That lack of results will completely demoralize even the smartest and hardest working individual. **It's human psychology:** the more time you spend on something with no reward, the harder it is to continue doing it.

Now, I have a question for you:

Are you worried the same will happen to you? Are you scared that you'll waste all your time on the pointless tasks that "job search experts" give as advice without even considering the obstacles you're facing?

Or worse: perhaps it has already happened to you, and you're tired of it?

If you say, "Heck, yeah Mike!" then you're in luck. What I have described is an unfortunate truth, but your personal experience does *not* have to follow that pattern. In the rest of this article I'm going to tell you the top three "time wasters" that lead to one feeling demotivated, unaccomplished and ready to quit.

The simple eliminate of these time wasters will dramatically alter your experience. If you follow through, **I believe YOU CAN BEAT THE ODDS.** Let's dive right in!

Time Waster #1 – Constantly Rewriting Your Resume

When I ask job-seekers how much time they spend on their resumes and cover letters, the answer is typically "I change it for almost every application."

This is not necessary!

Let me tell you something very important: your résumé is going to be looked at for about fifteen seconds, and your cover letter, maybe not at all.

That's all the time you have to impress your future employer.

Fifteen seconds.

So how do you stand out from the 100 other résumés they see?

Have an unbelievable great headline!

Spend time crafting the best headline you possibly can and THEN have 20 people read it. Ask them what they think. Get honest opinions, and perfect that headline. Then, make sure that every single bullet point on your resume is IMPRESSIVE. No one wants to read about your boring, day-to-day tasks.

Hiring managers want to see results.

Highlight the outstanding things you've done in your life: the successful projects or teams you've been on, the papers you have published, the conferences you have attended. Use strong, active verbs like "generated," "saved" or "increased." In fact, you need to make it look like they would be crazy not to hire you!

Now that you've done that work, I'm giving you permission to NEVER touch it again.

With these careful edits and selective bullet points, your resume will get noticed. You will also save yourself valuable hours that can now be devoted to more important things.

Time Waster #2 – Applying Online

Most international students and immigrants think it's enough to submit résumés online through job sites and their school's career services website, likely because this is what they see most American students do. In fact, when I was at school that's exactly what I did, too. Filled out the form, clicked 'submit,' and just hoped that it would work out.

Since then, I've realized that this is how FOOLS try to get jobs. This is not how I got my manager position at a Fortune 500 company at age 25. I was supposed to have 10 years of experience for the position, but I still managed to get the job. This "experience" obstacle that I encountered is somewhat similar scenario to work visa obstacle that international students face.

It's not the fact that you are under qualified for the position, rather most hiring managers are looking for a specific criteria that your résumé may not fit.

In my case it was experience. In your case, it's a U.S. work visa.

So how do you get around that type of obstacle? And how does this relate to online applications? Well, the most effective way to show a company that you can provide the skills and services they need is to speak to them in person. A conversation conveys much more than a cover letter. So:

YOU MEET PEOPLE FACE-TO-FACE.

The #1 best way to get a job is through networking. According to a source, almost 75% of jobs never even make it to job posting boards. This means that someone within the company, or a contact met by networking was able to secure the position before the company began to look to the general job market.

Your dream job may be LOOOOONGGG gone before you even had a chance to apply.

You're probably thinking that your own network of classmates, friends and relatives might be a good job source. Maybe you can just casually say, "Hey! I'm looking for a job. Can you help me?"

The vast majority of the time, these connections prove far too limited to be of any real assistance in an aggressive job search. More than likely, the connection that will lead to your dream job will be someone that you have not yet met. This person will be like Mihaela's contact in Chapter 1: someone in your "extended network" (connected to you by a 2nd or 3rd degree).

I hope you are now asking, "How do I meet these people?" This leads me to my next HUGE time-waster.

Time Waster #3 – Being Vague About Your Goal

Being extremely specific is the best way to get a job. You fail fast or succeed fast. When most people start looking for jobs, they look for extremely generic titles like "marketing manager," "engineer," or "business analyst."

This is *not* what you're going to do.

Instead, you're going to think about EXACTLY what you want to do. This means thinking about exactly what industry you want to be in, as well as the specific job title you want in that industry.

You are going to focus all of your energy on getting THAT job at one of your dream companies, **which means that you need to meet people at those companies.**

So What Is Your Dream Job?

Frequently when I asked my students, 'What is your dream job?" or "What do you want to do with your life?" I hear responses like,

"Well, I'm a marketing major so I think I'd like to work for a big tech company like Google or Amazon."

"Alright," I answer. "What position?"

"Probably something in the marketing department," the student tells me.

At this point, I have to be straight with my student. If you think in such vague, general terms your job search will be a hundred times harder, and you will likely feel much more discouraged along the way.

What you need is specificity. The last position that I held at a Fortune 500 company was 'Continuous Improvement Manager' of two manufacturing plants. 'Continuous Improvement Manager' is not a title that many people seek out. This makes the title easier for the right person (who has that specific title in mind) to get.

How did I pick that title?

My background is chemical engineering. At my first job, I became an expert in Lean Six Sigma. I loved improving current processes, changing procedures and creating new innovations. Building on this original interest of mine, I researched online and interviewed my contacts with similar backgrounds. In the end, I found four different titles that fit. "Continuous Improvement Manager" was one of those titles.

Now you need to do the same thing.

Don't worry—you don't have to find these titles on your won. In the blueprint, we will talk about how you can find them. Yes, it will take a little bit of research, this step will dramatically improve your success rate.

The Blueprint Process

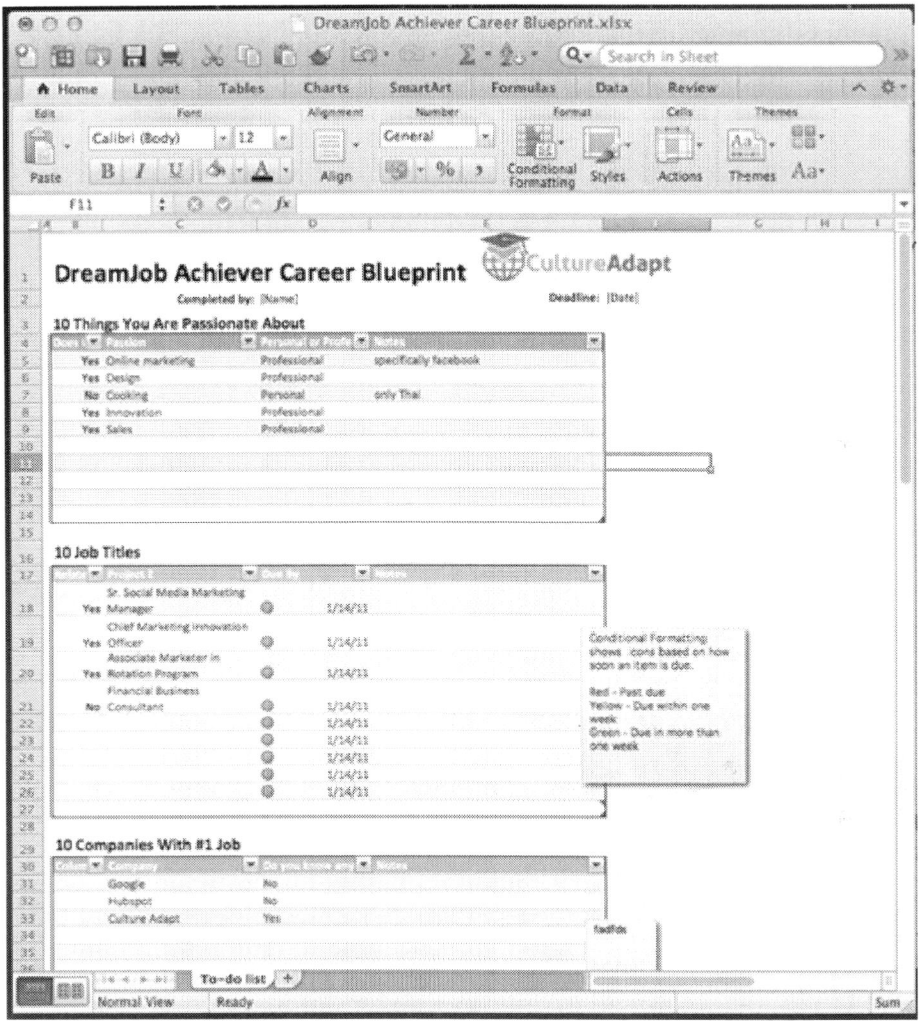

DreamJob Achiever Career Blueprint.xlsx
Search in Sheet
Home Layout Tables Charts SmartArt Formulas Data Review
Edit Font Alignment Number Format Cells Themes
Paste Calibri (Body) 12 Align General Conditional Formatting Styles Actions Themes
F11

DreamJob Achiever Career Blueprint CultureAdapt
Completed by: [Name] Deadline: [Date]

10 Things You Are Passionate About

Yes	Online marketing	Professional	specifically facebook
Yes	Design	Professional	
No	Cooking	Personal	only Thai
Yes	Innovation	Professional	
Yes	Sales	Professional	

10 Job Titles

Yes	Sr. Social Media Marketing Manager	1/14/11	
Yes	Chief Marketing Innovation Officer	1/14/11	
Yes	Associate Marketer in Rotation Program	1/14/11	
No	Financial Business Consultant	1/14/11	
		1/14/11	
		1/14/11	
		1/14/11	
		1/14/11	
		1/14/11	

Conditional Formatting shows icons based on how soon an item is due.
Red - Past due
Yellow - Due within one week
Green - Due in more than one week

10 Companies With #1 Job

	Google	No	
	Hubspot	No	
	Culture Adapt	Yes	

fadfds
To-do list
Normal View Ready Sum

This is the career blueprint. (download from www.cultureadapt.com/resources) This is your guide through your international career development journey.

How do you get started?

First you must figure out exactly what you want to do with your career. What are you passionate about? Write down ten personal and professional things you love on your Blueprint. It may be online marketing, sales, sports, cooking, languages: any one of these could be the spark that will keep you going.

Next, list out ten very specific job titles that involve your passions. This is going to require you to think a little bit, research online and ask people from your network.

Now it is time to narrow down your options. Pick the title of the one position you really, really, really want. It's important that you only pick one to pursue.

Take a moment to think about WHY this position is perfect for you. This is important. If you don't think about this, you may end up in a career you dislike. The main focus of your goal should be something you love, not a work visa. If your only focus is a visa, you won't be able to exemplify the characteristics that your employer is looking for.

After deciding on the position, it's time to figure out what it takes to be a perfect fit for that job. Interview people who have similar positions, research online, or ask mentors what it takes to be the **best person possible** for that position. This is precisely the kind of research that led me to successful job offers.

Now you're ready to find ten companies that have that position. One thing to remember is that the company may not have the position listed on their website or job postings. It may take some research (i.e. contacting the company by phone) to figure it out. Also, be aware that these companies could also be in a specific location, like New York, San Francisco, Boston, etc. You may need to take location into account. It is critical to only choose ten companies because if you choose more you will NOT BE focused enough.

In all honesty, unless you're spending 100% of your time job hunting, pursuing ten companies will feel like quite a lot of work. This is because you'll need to meet as many people as possible at those companies. The first thing you should do is check your LinkedIn contacts to see if you know anyone at those companies. LinkedIn is a great tool to use, allowing you to do much of your company research and offering an easy way to maintain contacts. If you notice a second or third-degree connection, you can ask to be introduced directly through the LinkedIn site. This is a great way to meet the "right" people. A similar online source of connectivity is Twitter. You can start following company contacts. Of course, you can return to traditional contacts like professors or university classmates, ask mentors or attend in-person networking events. Your task is to do whatever it takes to meet those people.

One final option is to request an "informational interviews" with someone. This very powerful method will be discussed later in the book.

I'm not suggesting that you go to a networking event every day. As it happens, I often hear, "I go to networking events five nights a week but I still can't get a job."

In this case, someone is either going to the *wrong* networking events, or he doesn't know *who* to meet. Going to a networking event without a goal in mind can be a waste of time and energy. With literally thousands of networking events every month, in every city, it is easy to get off-track. Don't get completely lost: focus on *your* specific goal.

During the next four weeks and beyond, you will continue to improve your communication skills. This training will allow you to do really well on that interview. When you already know what makes you **the perfect candidate** for the job, all you have to do is express it to the right people. At this point, you will already have enough contacts inside the company that you'll basically get the job on the spot!

Throughout the rest of the book I'll teach you ways to meet these people and build relationships to attain you dream job.

Blueprint Flowchart

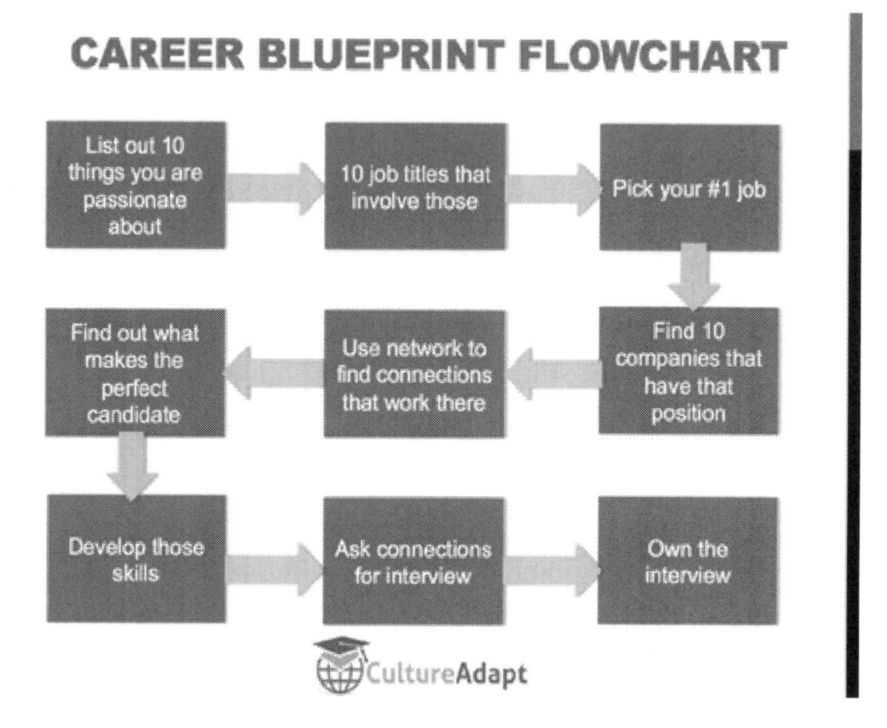

Being an engineer, I like to use flowcharts. If you're a visual learner like me, this is an easy breakdown of the Blueprint. Here are the nine steps:

1 - List out 10 things that you are passionate about
2 - List out 10 job titles that involve your passions
3 - Pick your number one job
4 - Find 10 companies that have that position in them
5 - Use your network to find connections that work at those companies
6 - Find out what will make you the perfect candidate
7 - Develop the necessary skills
8 - Ask the right people to get you an interview
9 - Ace the interview

Using Mentors to Improve the Process

A friend and former student of mine with a background in audit approached me and said, "Mike, my dream job is at PWC."

Without thinking for second I said, "Alright! Great! Let me see what I can do."

I immediately checked my LinkedIn and personal contacts for people I knew at PWC. It only took about me two emails to get his resume into the right hands.

He was able to bypass the entire online applicant system, have his résumé referred and found himself with a great opportunity to get a job and an H-1B.

If you can build up a network of mentors like he has (professionals who have your best interests in mind and will go out of their way to help you) then your chance of success is greater.

Perhaps you could think of these mentors as employees or coworkers: you get a lot done yourself, but imagine there were five of you! Five people who have similar goals and motivations! You can get a heck of a lot more done this way. Build your own cooperative network like this, and you will see that it is extremely powerful.

Another benefit of the mentor-support is the amazing networks they have access to. People who have twenty or thirty years of successful business experience will have prolific networks which may connect you to hiring managers. These individuals accelerate the application process. Thus, by working through a few different people, you can reach your end goal finding an introduction to the person able to hire your at your dream job.

Though this may sound impossible right now, it is a lot easier than you would think. Perhaps you have an introduction from a friend: you can then meet this contact for lunch or to get coffee. This casual meet-up is a very common business practice. At this stage, it is not an interview. You are free to discuss a wider range of topics—topics that may even be off-limits during a tradition interview. You, too, will be able to express yourself more comfortably, as the experience will be less stressful. Then, at the later interview, you will feel even more confident in your abilities, and secure in your status as the best candidate.

How can you become the best candidate?

Many students believe that the process of proving one's value begins and ends in the interview room. In actuality, you should reveal your skills and experience to the company over time through networking. That way, the interview becomes more of a discussion of your value at the company, rather than a show-and-tell of all your past achievements. In this way, you can highlight in the interview those aspects that make you most qualified—even if that doesn't include years of experience or a prestigious degree.

In my case, I needed 10 years of experience to get the Dean Foods position. However, because I showed my abilities (which were valuable to the company even without years of experience behind them), the shortcomings were overlooked. The only way to manage this, though, is to *meet people prior to the interview.* Also bear in mind the challenges faced by the hiring managers. What worries do they have? What problems are you trying to solve? What responsibilities must they meet? Really get in their head, do a little bit of mind-reading. The number one question the hiring manager will ask is "Why should I hire you?"

This most well-known, infamous question must have an answer. It is up to you to prepare the most detailed, useful answer and *do the hiring manager's job for him!* Imagine that you walk into the interview, complete the question-and-answer and they hiring manager concludes with that simple question. Now imagine that you pull out a document details what you will be able to do within the first thirty, sixty or ninety days. To the hiring manager, this is an easily-read sign that shows you've already researched the company, the position and you know exactly what you will get done for that company. That's really powerful. From the point of view of the hiring manager, I can easily say that if you do this, you are in the top 1% of those interviewed. Right now, you may be asking:

What if I don't know what I want to do with my life?

What if i don't know who to reach out to?

What if I don't have enough experience?

What if...?

First, let me tell you that this kind of questioning, this attention to detail is a useful concern. It shows me that you are thinking about it the right way to approach this. You aren't wasting energy on thoughts about where to cut corners online, or how to accomplish all of this without having to meet new people or branch out. No, you're thinking in a strategic way that will help you get the job.

To help you with your planning, I'm going to give you the DreamJob Achiever Career Blueprint document. This template you can fill out step-by-step. Each note provides information on how to carry out different aspects of your own blueprint. Later in the book, I will address the specifics of this blueprint in greater detail. It's very easy to use, and great for encouraging you to maintain your very concentrated strategy to find the exact job, the exact company and the exact people you need to meet.

The 80/20 Rule

Pareto's principle, also known as the 80-20 rule, states that for many events, 80% of the effects result from 20% of causes. The rule is used in business, manufacturing, sales, economics, health, software and many other fields.

I can also tell you from personal experience that if you analyze your own life and apply the 80-20 rule, you will see that its application here, too. Once you are aware of those 'causal' factors, you can begin to streamline your approach. This will simplify every aspect of your life, removing waste-time. In turn, you will see better effective results.

For instance, I realized that I was only using 20% of my belongings 80% of the time, so got rid of everything I didn't use. It made my living space much cleaner, got me some extra cash and I have not missed anything that I got rid of. I work on maintaining this balance too, so you'll never see me wasting money buying things that I won't routinely use.

Similarly, with my finances, I figured out the 20% of my activities that I was spending 80% of my money on and cut it significantly. With my customers, I focus on the 20% that lead to 80% of my revenue.

So how does this apply to getting a job?

It all comes back to my point about being extremely specific. If you really focus and think about everything you're doing, you'll realize that 80% of your results are coming from 20% of your efforts.

Once you realize what that 20% is, you can eliminate all your non-value added (NVA) activities. As I mentioned, this will include constantly updating your resume and cover letter, applying to hundreds of jobs online and asking your existing network to help get you a job. Follow this one principle and you will see results.

Self-Assessment Time

One part of developing your career is going to be figuring out what your weaknesses and strengths are.

You have to be brutally honest with yourself and realize what you're good at—as well as what you're not. Once you establish what those weaknesses are, you have to schedule actions every single day to improve them. There is no quick way to improve: it simply takes dedication and constant action.

To help you in your self-improvement journey, I have created a very simple self-assessment tool to rate yourself and track your progress. (download from www.cultureadapt.com/resources) Here is an example:

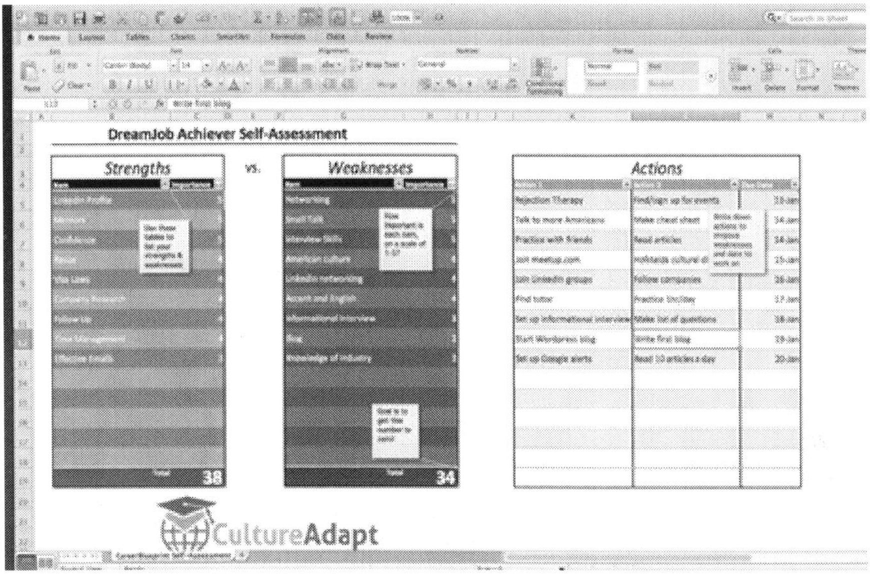

On this example, I have things like a LinkedIn profile, mentor network, confidence, resume, visa laws, company research, follow up, small talk, accent and English. These are all great skills to have on the "strengths" side. Of course you can list whatever is most relevant to you; these are ideas for you to start with.

The next part of your self-assessment is to rank your weaknesses in order the importance on a scale of one to five, with 'five' being most important. If we look at your weaknesses, networking and small talk are at the top (ranked 'five) because it is extremely important for you to build those skills to meet the "right" people and confidently converse with them.

I tell all of my students to think back to the 80/20 rule and work on improving their English conversational skills because this will improve many of their career skills at once (informational interviews, blogging, networking, etc.)

How much do you work to improve your weaknesses?

You want to work on them until they become strengths. Then you can take them off the "weaknesses" side and throw them on the "strengths" side. Your goal should be to get that weakness number down to zero.

You can accomplish this by taking action. The far right column serves as a place for you to record and track the different actions that you will take to improve. They don't have to be major accomplishments. On the contrary, small, daily actions like: "Talk to a stranger" or "practice introducing myself in front of a mirror" can prove much more helpful. Accomplishing something daily will give you a feeling of satisfaction, confidence and achievement that will help you remain positive in your job search. Regardless of the size of the action, that improvement will stay with you for your entire life.

The Network Paradox

I mentioned earlier that your existing network probably won't be able to put you in touch with the *right* people, though they might be able to connect you with someone who can help you along your way. These connections, though somewhat removed, can still prove very useful in the long run.

It is your task to unearth your existing network. Once you have established who you can reach out to, you need to begin building those connections. Only then can the connections become valuable assets capable of opening doors.

Take a moment to imagine that you actually sitting down for coffee with the hiring manager at your dream company. It does have a little more appeal than an impersonal online application, right? During that coffee meet-up with your inside connection, you need to be looking for information about what the company needs and expects from its employees. With this information, you have the opportunity to mold yourself into the best candidate for that position. For example, is the company looking for experience in a very specific niche? Is it looking for someone who has worked on a diverse team with different backgrounds? Maybe the company is looking for someone bilingual, or for someone with the ability to lead a team project, or do online marketing. You really have to get as specific as possible: only with an awareness of these details will you be able to meet them. Just keep differentiation in mind right now. This isn't the time to apply online, or take the steps that others do. Right now you are trying to overcome the hurdle of being an international individual in need of a visa and a job—the latter being hard enough on its own.

How to Differentiate Yourself

As I said before, differentiating yourself is about moving away from the common, expected approaches to getting a job. These passive approaches can lead to that feeling of nonfulfillment and defeat, and that's when you begin to think about giving up. After all, a person can only hear 'no' so many times! I have personally had this experience in my first company: at the start, my efforts to make a sale were met with a continuous stream of 'no, no, *no.*' It was completely demoralizing, and nearly convinced me to end my venture. The very same situation can arise when job hunting. You may have submitted one hundred résumés, or cold-called one hundred companies, and have had no results. Nothing. Even if you arrange an interview, you still don't receive a call back. When you begin to expect that response, you may begin to avoid that situation altogether, for fear of rejection. Luckily, you're not going to take that approach this time. Instead, you will focus on being undeniably, spectacularly useful and unique. Only then will you be noticed.

Before we move on, I want to look at the concept of 'fear of rejection.' While it isn't pleasant, in the business world (and in life in general) you *will be* rejected. There is a lot you can do to avoid that rejection, but ultimately, not everyone will say 'yes.' It's useful to prepare yourself mentally for those occasional refusals, with different kinds of activities that you can do. I have compiled a book of ideas for you, which will push you to *try* to get rejected every single day, for thirty days in a row. Over time, you will build a thick skin, and the occasional rejection will not be so devastating to your overall feelings of confidence. The only way to train yourself, though, is to actually follow through with these exercises. Day-by-day, step-by-step. If you aren't diligent, you won't see the results. Attempting to follow a thirty-day program like this can cause a negativity loop: you will feel motivated to begin, then discouraged if you don't finish—often even more discouraged and self-conscious than when you began. The only option, then, is to fully follow through!

Your sense of rejection may not even be so direct as hearing 'no.' I'm sure that you read information about job prospects for international students, or the economic downturn, and feel like the whole world is saying 'no.' You might see a negative article like this one from *The Cornel Sun Newspaper,* which states that "…the number of jobs available to international students has been decreasing, because employers are not as strapped for talent as they were before the economic downturn two years ago."

This quote is quite disheartening, but fortunately, it is just not true. Just as many visas are given out this year as there were two years ago, and just as many companies are looking for talent. In fact, I would say even more companies are **looking for global talent** than they were before because the world is becoming more global.

As you can see, there will always be negative information regarding your situation. You have to be careful about what you accept as fact. True, some articles make legitimate points, but not every single bit of pessimistic news needs to be acknowledged.
You have to remember that positive action will produce results: when you are passionate, take initiative and count on yourself, your likelihood of success is much greater.

What Employers Are Looking For in Recruits

I'll briefly go over a few things that most employers look for in recruits to give you some more ideas of skills you can improve.

1. Problem-solving skills
That doesn't mean just math, but anything that has to do with problems (on paper, in person or otherwise).

2. Being able to think on your feet
Memorization skills and knowledge of useful information will come in handy, but it must be coupled with an ability to work with any given situation. Have you ever heard the term 'book smart'? It refers to someone who has a vast store of knowledge—who can, for example, list the first fifty prime numbers and explain the current political debate on fossil fuels, but who doesn't remember to look both ways before crossing the street. Remember that situational awareness and an ability to adapt to new people and circumstances will be just as useful as any information you study in a textbook.

3. Ability to think outside the box
Any employee can continue to do what his predecessor did. A truly valuable employee provides innovative ideas, and propels the company forward.

4. A balanced IQ and EQ (Emotional Intelligence Quotient)
This ties in with your communication skills and your ability to 'think on your feet.' Hiring managers want to see that you have both intelligences and practical skills, as well as 'people skills': an ability to work with others, a sense of personal responsibility and accountability, etc.

5. Team-working skills

As I just mentioned in the previous point, interaction is crucial. Most likely, you will be working with multiple people in a team atmosphere. Your understanding of American personal and professional culture will be play a role, as well as your ability to learn new habits, ways of communicating, problem-solving skills, and so on. The group dynamic is always difficult to balance, and hiring managers look for employees who can handle it.

6. Passion

I keep returning to the idea of passion, because I can't say it enough times. Employers love to see motivated employees (because this often implies that the employee with be hard-working, and personally motivated to do well).

7. Great work ethic and dedication

The skills and traits I have mentioned all add up to a potentially great employee. The one thing that will solidify that status is simple *hard work.* In the United States, this attitude will be respected, and rewarded.

Questions and Actions

If I have questions about the career blueprint what should I do?

You should find a peer or professional mentor to evaluate it for you. It's always good to get feedback! You can also post it to the Culture Adapt Facebook, Twitter or LinkedIn Group (International Career Development) and ask for feedback.

I'm trying to find networking events in my target industry but the industry is not big and there aren't many events. How can I expand the chance to connect to the right people?

This is a great question and goes back to getting really specific about your dream job title and the ten companies you're targeting. Those specifics can feel limiting, but will help you in the long run. Go back to your LinkedIn connections and search for connections once more—perhaps you missed something at first. Then, you can ask for an introduction or directly connect with these new contacts. Ask if they're attending any networking events in the near future.

Your e-mail to one of your future co-workers could look something like this:

> Hi (First Name),
> I would love to meet someone at your company to find out a little more about the company culture and what a "day in the life" is like. Are there any events coming up that you or other employees are going to attend?
> Regards,
> Michael

You can also call the company directly and talk to the front desk person or human resources. People are generally open and talkative in America, and shouldn't have a problem telling you what you need to know. Who knows? You might even get invited to one of their private events.

What if I still can't find any?

The short answer: you're probably not trying hard enough, so as to avoid intimidating conversations with strangers.

But for argument's sake let's say that isn't the case. Perhaps you're in the-middle-of-nowhere, hours away from the nearest city. You can completely bypass networking events altogether and just offer to take someone out to coffee or lunch. This can be even better than networking events because you will have their undivided attention. In a situation like this, I love to get the employee to speak about their own experiences with questions like:

"How did you become so successful?"

"How did you land your awesome job in the first place?"

What if I'm not confident in my networking skills?

Practice, practice, practice. Remember the rejection therapy ideas? Building your networking skills is extremely important and we're going to give you some tips and tricks for build them later in the book.

Again, if a crowded room is too intimidating, you can always ask for a one-on-one coffee meeting with someone. This interaction may build your confidence in your conversational English so that next time, you have the courage to walk up and talk to anyone at a networking event.

I don't have twitter, do I need an account?

Yes. Not having a twitter was a mistake I made early in my career. It's extremely easy to start conversations with people and companies you don't know personally. You can follow anyone or any company on twitter and have an open conversation with them. If you're trying to find events you could even tweet at them:

"Hey any fun industry networking events coming up?"

I want to do something that is outside of my major. What can I do?

Again, most visas are very particular about having to do with what you're studying at school. In order for you to get an H-1B visa, you have to show that you are an expert in the field you want to work in and usually that means having a degree in that field.

However, there *are* success stories of people doing this so again, I'd suggest going to an immigration attorney if you're in this situation.

Another suggestion I have is to combine your passions. For example, let's say you studied finance but are really passionate about fashion. A potential solution? You can try to get a job in the finance department at a fashion magazine or well-known clothing brand.

Tools & Tricks

Google Reader & Alerts - These two amazing tools can be used to learn about the industry and companies you are interested in. Simply type in keywords that you want and they will send you e-mail updates every day with relevant articles.

MyVisaJobs (www.myvisajobs.com) - A comprehensive list of companies that have sponsored a visa in the past. You can sort it by industry, company size, number of visas applied for, etc. You can narrow down what companies you're looking at, too, keeping in mind that if a company sponsors a lot of visas every year, there's a very high chance that they will do so again this year. In all, it's a really useful tool.

Asana (www.asana.com) - Task manager to help you manage your life and monitor your progress.

Crunchbase (www.crunchbase.com) - Free database of technology companies, people, and investors.

TechCrunch (www.techcrunch.com) - All the tech news you could ever want. TechCrunch provides a source of information about growing companies.

Alltop (www.alltop.com) - Online magazine rack that serves as a directory of the web's top blogs and news sources based on category. Just type in your field or industry into the search bar at the top, and Alltop will recommend categories for you to choose from.

MarketWatch (www.marketwatch.com) - Great starting point for more quantifiable information about your target industry.

Skoll World Forum (www.skollworldforum.org) - Interesting site that allows you to follow trends in the social entrepreneurship.

Technorati (**www.technorati.com**) - One of the most well-know blog directories.

Personal Challenge

Be More Productive (1 Day)

Tonight, write down one or two of your most important tasks to be completed the next day. Immediately after waking the next day, complete your tasks one at a time with absolutely no interruptions. That means no Facebook, no e-mails, no procrastinating. Just do what you have set out to do. It will help to make these your most important tasks (and most dreaded) because then you will have more pressure to accomplish them.

This is a trick I use everyday to increase my productivity. Psychologically it makes you feel like your day has already been successful. When I wasn't doing this, I not only felt less productive, but I did get less done. Also, by completing these tasks first your mind doesn't wander throughout the day, overwhelmed by all the things you need to get done.

For example, let's say that you hate writing your résumé, or improving the existing one. Still, you know you have to do it. If you don't do it first thing in the morning you're going to be constantly thinking about it the rest of the day. You might even subconsciously waste time with unimportant tasks to avoid taking care of it.

Many people I know wake up and immediately check their e-mail. This becomes completely devastating to their productivity, because they find themselves confronted with all of these little "emergencies" in their inbox. Then the focus is on these "emergencies," instead of the truly important tasks. Ultimately, they can find themselves at the end of the day, feeling as though they have accomplished nothing.

That's not what we want. We want you to feel like you make progress towards your goal every single day. For that reason, you must stick to the career blueprint.

Part 2:
The Throw

"Do you want to know who you are? Don't ask. Act! Action will delineate and define you." – *Thomas Jefferson*

Chapter 4 - Take Action

"Life begins at the end of your comfort zone." *Neale Donald Walsch*

Making BIG Moves From 5500 Kilometers Away

Eva dreamed moving to America after graduation. Her boyfriend lived in Boston and that's where she aimed to be. She hoped to get a job at a large corporation, startup or possibly start her own company. There was just one minor obstacle that stood in her way...she lived in Rotterdam, in the Netherlands.

She hadn't even attended school in America, but this didn't stop her from following her dream. Instead, it merely incentivized her to work even harder. Thus, she became valedictorian of her undergraduate class at Rotterdam University, founded a charitable organization, and pursued a Master's degree to build her expertise in Tax Law & Economics.

As graduation approached, she decided to plan a trip to America to chase her dream (despite having little idea how to get a job in America). As her trip neared she had many questions surrounding the process and decided to look for help. She looked on websites, asked for advice from friends, but nothing really seemed to answer all her questions. She was about to give up when she stumbled on an online class, Dream Job Achiever, that guaranteed assistance in finding a job and visa in America, in just four weeks. She decided to take a chance, and signed up.

Before she knew it, she was taking action in ways that were completely different from the business culture she grew up in. She approached peers and asked to be connected to decision makers at her target companies. She was making phone calls to American companies to set up informational interviews, e-mailing people she'd never met, and using her extended network on LinkedIn to meet the "right" people. In fact, during the four week period her LinkedIn network grew by 400%! (99 to 415 contacts)

Sure enough, just three weeks later she had been internally recommended at three of her target companies and had 5+ informational meetings scheduled in Boston!

Eva had done the seemingly-impossible. She had scheduled interviews at American companies before ever stepping foot in The States. Even in her excitement, she was initially shocked. Soon she realized, though, that it wasn't so surprising: she had taken action, and achieved results.

Why People Don't Take Action

Your career blueprint is done. You know the exact position you want, and you've found companies have that position. Now, you need to meet the right people at those companies. But you aren't just meeting a peer, or a casual acquaintance. Those 'right' people are company decision-makers, with much more experience and much more control in the situation. That can be very intimidating—so much so that some get so scared that they never take action.

Here the top three reasons why people don't take action:

Reason #1 - 'What If' Paralysis

People start asking themselves questions like,

"What if this company doesn't like me?"

"What if this person doesn't want to talk to me?"

"What if I'm not a good fit for this job?"

"What if I don't have enough experience?"

I call this *'What If' paralysis.* If you don't overcome this mindset, you will never take action. Many people struggle with this DAILY, in all aspects of their lives. They constantly worry what others will think of them and their actions. Doing this will stop you from achieving great things.

To overcome this fear you must first acknowledge that you do this *constantly*. Become aware of the exact moment when you begin entering the paralysis. Once you can isolate this moment, you can try to break the habit by taking swift action without overthinking it. Stay positive, forget your fears, forget what other people will think about you and **JUST ACT.**

Reason #2 - The Network Paradox

Everyone has built up a network over the years of family, high school friends, college classmates, acquaintances, teachers and co-workers. Everyone thinks that by tapping into that network they are taking action. Unfortunately, this will not get you a job. So why do we still do this?

Because it's easy. This is what I call the "network paradox": it seems like such an accessible source of contacts, but it is often quite limiting. You need to actively seek out second and third connections, as well as completely new connections, to break out of this paradox. Become a little more spontaneous, talk to people you don't know and open yourself up to serendipity. You never know who is going to be able to help you.

Reason #3 - It's Comfortable in Your Comfort Zone

Most people don't enjoy doing things outside of their comfort zone. Again, it's easier and feels safer. Attending the same events week after week, talking to people of the same age and status, going to the same place everyday for lunch...it's nice, right?

Wrong. Comfortable, maybe, but this behavior will never lead to new opportunities.

Life should be a challenge. Push yourself to try something new every day. It can be a new food, walking a new route home, going to a different bar than usual, a new event or trying something you're scared of (personally, I enjoy jumping out of planes). When you push your everyday then you are actually going to see more results than anyone else.

The Wrong Actions

Now that your mind is in the right place, you're probably ready to take TONS of action! But before you do, make sure you are not taking the *wrong* actions. The wrong actions could be going to as many networking events as possible, applying online as much as possible or e-mailing as many contacts as possible and saying, "Hey can you help me get a job?"

If your action is not specifically connected to your targets, it will be a waste of time and energy. Even I have fallen prey to this. When I was starting my first company, I just wanted to meet as many people as I could and network as much as I could. I went to networking event after networking event, hoping to meet people that could help grow my business. Guess what happened?

I ended up wasting a lot of time and energy. Because I didn't know exactly who to meet on the events, it was draining and unhelpful. You don't need to make the same mistake.

The Right Action #1 - Finding Mentors

Mentors are key to your lifelong success. A mentor should always give you honest feedback, providing opinions and advice when others might not take the time to help. They will give you access to their network and resources, wanting to see you succeed. Ultimately, they can help you in all aspects of your life.

Over the last six years, one of my greatest mentors has inspired dramatic growth in me both professionally and personally. She is always extremely honest with me. If my work isn't up to par, she tells me: "It needs work." If I do something very well, she tells me, "I'm proud of you." If I ask her something via e-mail and she doesn't agree, I get no response. Our relationship has developed to the point of most efficient communication, and her guidance has been invaluable.

Advice from mentors shortens your learning curve significantly. For example, if you're mentor is someone successful from your specific industry, they can teach you their proven strategies to help you become successful more quickly. They will tell you the things that were incredibly hard for them to learn thereby shortening the time it takes you to learn. They can also help you identify and improve your weaknesses.

So how do you make sure that you have find good mentors? What are the traits you should look for?

You're not just looking for someone who is older than you or has more experience than you. You want to foster a relationship with someone who is going to continually be a good mentor to you. They should be willing to share their skills and expertise for free. They should actually want to help you and take a personal interest in your success. They will go out of their way to help you find the connections that are going to get you the job. You also want a mentor that's going to demonstrate a positive attitude. If your mentor is often negative, constantly saying bad things about other people or situations, they are probably not a good choice. A great mentor is going to be open to hearing other people's opinions because it will help them continue to grow. A great mentor will love continual learning in their field and will be open to hearing anyone's feedback, including your own.

They will also give you constructive feedback. For example, if you bring them your résumé, they won't just say, "it's good" or "it's bad." Instead, they offer suggestions, and encourage your fine-tuning of it. Finding mentors who can motivate you will help you work harder, faster and more often.

So now that you know what a good mentor should act like, I'll explain the different types of mentors. The greater variety of mentors with whom you work, the bigger your network will become and the more easily you will get a job.

Type of Mentor: Informal
95% of mentors are informal which simply means that there is no agreement in writing. There is no agreement on either side about the number of times you meet or talk. The relationship has formed naturally throughout time and this person eventually becomes your mentor.

Type of Mentor: Formal
Examples of these would be career services at a school, a boss at work or a board member of your company. This type of mentor has some kind of formal agreement in writing and possibly an agreement on how much time you're going to spend with each other and how much help you'll get.

Type of Mentor: Role Model
Someone in your field that you want to emulate. You can copy their strategies and things that they've done to become successful. This will shorten your learning curve.

Type of Mentor: Developmental
Someone who is going to give you feedback on your skills, and how you can develop those skills for you to get a job. This will go back to the strengths and weaknesses assessment formulated on your career blueprint.

Type of Mentor: Peer Mentor
This could be a classmate, friend or a colleague at work. Whoever it happens to be, this person is at roughly the same level as you in the professional world. I would suggest finding a number of peer mentors because they're great people to ask for daily advice. You could critique each other's résumé, interview skills, networking skills, etc.

Type of Mentor: Reciprocal Mentor
Someone that is helping you in return for your help. You could be helping each other find the connections that will eventually get you both jobs. That relationship has strong incentive for each sides to provide what the other needs.

Getting The Best Mentors

Your mentor system will significantly speed up the process of finding the right connections. Sometimes you might even have a really powerful mentors who have the ability to offer you a job. With this in mind, always "reach for the stars" when forming your network of mentors. You needn't settle for a mentor whose advice and contributions are mediocre. Try to find someone whose intelligence, career and life approach you really respect. From there, it is only a matter of taking the next step towards your career in America.

Now, when trying to recruit a mentor, it is not good to be blunt. Asking, "Will you be my mentor?" or "Can you help me get a job?" Will generally put people off. Instead, try to be mores subtle. Ask about the person's own career and experience, and lead into the suggestion of a mentor relationship. A question that I always ask potential mentors is:

"How did you become successful?"

When you ask someone that, they're probably going to start teaching you something immediately. People like to talk about things they've learned throughout life to become successful. So if you can get someone to open up and start talk about that, that's the start of a good mentor relationship.

You can also ask for a quick meeting or phone call on a specific topic. When you are first trying to build that relationship, it's important to not take up a lot of their time. I've done that in the past for things like social media marketing, online webinars, sales, etc. I just ask someone:

"Hey, I have a question about this that's just going to take about 15 minutes of your time."

This approach gets a much higher response rate than saying, "Hey, can I sit down for you with an hour to discuss my career goals?" That's a question to ask a long-time mentor. Also, as I've previously mentioned, you should be focused on helping others as much as possible, and that includes mentors. When a mentor is really successful on his own, it can be hard to figure out how you can help them. Don't give up! Try to think "outside the box."

The Right Action #2 - Find The Correct Networking Events

I briefly mentioned that you can *waste* time at networking events. It's important that you research events before attending, mainly focusing on the question of value: is this going to help me achieve my overall goal? You have to make sure the industry for the event is actually the one that you are looking for. There are hundreds of networking events offered, and if you're not going to the right industry events then probably you're not going to meet the right people. If you decided that it will help you, figure out how, *specifically.* Ask yourself:

"What is my goal for this event?"

Again, this ties back to your blueprint. Is your plan to meet ten people from one company or one person from ten companies? Is it to meet the hiring manager or the founder of a company? One trick that I use to help myself choose good events is to check the guest list. A lot of event websites now list out the people attending the event because it provides social validity and proof of legitimacy. You can target specific people that you want to meet that way. The last question I ask is:

"Are people talking about this event?"

Twitter, Facebook, LinkedIn, local news sources, and the event page will show you just how much 'buzz' exists around this particular event. You will often see hype on an event page or registration page, and then no one shows up. You need to go to outside sources for more accurate information. Some people also think that because an event is expensive, it is worthwhile. This is not true. You still have to make sure that the event is in line with your goals.

16 Best Websites to Find Professional Events*

These are the websites that I use the most to find networking events. There are many more out there but these are enough for you to start with. Remember, stay focused.

1 Eventbrite.com
2 Allconferences.com
3 Google
4 Yelp.com
5 Craigslist
6 Lanyrd.com
7 Internations.org
8 Nationalcareerfairs.com
9 Twitter
10 Facebook
11 Meetup.com
12 LinkedIn Groups
13 Eventful.com
14 Zvents.com
15 Netparty.com

16 Asmallworld.net

*Listed in no specific order of usefulness

The Allconferences.com database provides information on any conference, in any industry. Conferences are really a great place to meet a lot of people and typically, conferences will draw in people in higher ranking positions. I've been to a number of very cool conferences and met CEO's of giant companies. That being the case, it is important that when you go to those events you aren't afraid of approaching anyone. If you see someone famous in the business world, you need to be able to walk right up to them and say:

"Hey, how is it going? I really respect you and your career." (then give your 30-second elevator pitch).

Internations.org is a world-wide expat network. Here you'll find a large number of foreign nationals who have been successful in America. These people have experience in finding employment and applying for visas, and would potentially be great mentors.

Nationalcareerfairs.com is a great way to find career fairs outside of your school or university.

LinkedIn groups are another amazing way to find industry events. Join as many targeted LinkedIn groups as you can. You can join 52 groups so I would suggest you find 52 that will align with your blueprint.

The Right Action #3 - Informational Interviews

This is the easiest way to get inside the company. It also happens to be one of the most underutilized tools in a job seekers repertoire. An information interview is valuable because it allows you to speak with a possible employer in a calm, no-pressure environment. Such a meet-up can be arranged with anyone in an organization who will agree to it: a new hire, manger, the hiring manager or even the CEO. You can ask about company culture, about the job, about how someone might get the job, or how that person became successful. It's very relaxed and it is a great way to start establishing a relationship with the right people.

Now you may be asking how you can arrange an interview like this. You can use your existing network to ask for introductions to your 2nd and 3rd connections. Another option is to search LinkedIn and connect with people at your target companies (yes, it's ok to do this without ever meeting the connection). You can ask people that you met at networking events, or mentors for introductions. There are many different options.

Don't think that you have to start with the hiring manager either. You can start up someone that has a similar position to the one you want and interview them. Then ask them to introduce you to someone else. Your goal should be to eventually sit down with the decision-maker, but it doesn't have to start there.

When asking someone for an informational interview you need to find out what is most convenient for them: a phone call, or an in-person meeting. You can even offer to take them out to lunch or coffee, both common offers to someone in America (be aware, though, that asking someone to dinner is *not).* Also keep in mind that the timing and duration of this meeting are at the discretion of the employee. You need to be accommodating, because this person is doing you a favor and sharing his or her time.

15 Great Informational Interview Questions

1. Can you tell me how you reached this position? What's the company culture like?

2. What do you like most about what you do, and what would you change if you could?

3. How do people break into this field?

4. What are the types of jobs that exist where you work and in the industry in general?

5. Where would you suggest a person investigate if the person were particularly skilled at (fill in the blank – quantitative thinking, communications, writing, advocacy)?

6. What does a typical career path look like in your industry?

7. What are some of the biggest challenges facing your company and your industry today?

8. Are there any professional or trade associations I should connect with?

9. What do you read—in print and online—to keep up with developments in your field?

10. How do you see your industry changing in the next 10 years?

11. If you were just getting involved now, where would you put yourself?

12. What's a typical day like for you?

13. What's unique or differentiating about your company?

14. How has your job (starting a blog, running a company, etc.) differed from your expectations? What have been the greatest moments and biggest challenges?

15. What are some important skills to develop for this industry and position?

How to get an informational interview

Informational interviews are one of the most underutilized tools in a job seekers repertoire. Most people don't know how to get them or what the heck one is. You should know that they are very common, extremely valuable, and you can have an informational interview WITH ANYONE.

It is a great way to build a relationship with someone at your dream company that may eventually help get you a real interview. It provides a low stress environment for both you and the company employee, where there is no expectation of employment. Rather, you are just gathering information. You can ask about the company culture, the interview process, traits they look for in applicants and how to be successful.

Sounds great, right? It is. And getting an informational interview shouldn't be tough. You can ask via e-mail, LinkedIn message or by just calling the company and asking. Have a look at the simple email template that I often used to get informational interviews.

> Hi (First Name),
> I was hoping to connect so I could find out more about your awesome job and success!
> I'm a (industry or title) specialist with a (major) degree, striving to succeed in the industry like you have.
> If you could spare a couple minutes, I'd love to have a quick phone call to ask a couple questions. (or buy you lunch/coffee if you have more time)
> What day/time in the next week would work for you?
> Thanks in advance!
> Your Name
> P.S. – (something that will help them)

Notice that my aim is concise and it is clear what I'm asking for. I will either get a 'yes' or 'no' reply. You'll notice I also avoid the phrase 'let me know when you are available.' I don't use this because it doesn't force someone to take action. You want to give some kind of deadline—some specific timeframe.

The postscript (P.S.) isn't necessary but can be powerful. Most people will read the P.S. even if they don't read the rest of the email. People naturally tend to believe that postscripts have important information in them, and will therefore take a look. This gives you the ideal opportunity to try to help your reader in some way. Perhaps you share an interesting industry article, or upcoming event.

Finally, when addressing the email, I typically use someone's first name. I would only use Mr.__ or Ms.__ if it's a very important person, or if that person is much older than me.

The Right Action #4 - Attend Career Fairs

Another great way to take action is by attending career fairs. Every school has their own career fair, but you are going to go one step further. You will attend other school's career fairs, as well as professional career fairs associated with your industry.

To be successful at a career fair, you can't just walk in and hand people your résumé. You need to make recruiters respect and remember you. I've seen people walk into a fair in jeans and t-shirt, hand their résumé to a recruiter and then a second later, I watch as the recruiter tosses the résumé in the garbage. You really have to make a strong impression to even have a chance.

One way to make an impression is with a perfected personal elevator pitch. I go over this later in the book but basically in 30-60 seconds, you need to be able to convey who you are personally, professionally, and why you are different from every other potential employee at the fair. My advice for perfecting this pitch is to practice in front of a mirror until it's amazing. Again, I will cover this in-depth in a later chapter.

Another important aspect to your first-impression is your appearance. Quite simply, you have to look good. Be dressed the way you want to be perceived: a responsible, mature professional. This doesn't mean that you have to look 'bland' or 'safe.' I like to wear a conversation piece: something a little flashy like a cool tie, a cool watch, school ring, or necklace. Anything that could start a conversation and get a recruiter talking to you a little more than the 500 other people that day.

Before the event you should make a list of questions for specific companies. Do your research, find out which companies you want to speak to at the event and then tailor questions to each. If you have a list of very smart questions to ask these recruiters, that will show them that you're an intelligent, hard-working individual worth remembering. By taking thirty minutes to write down some great questions, you will significantly differentiate yourself.

The last thing you need to do to be successful is to follow-up. That means you need to get the recruiter's contact information. Sometimes recruiters at career fairs will say they don't have contact information on them, but don't listen to that. Everyone carries business cards and even if they repeatedly say, "I don't have a business card," politely insist that they write down their e-mail on your notepad so you may send them a thank you.

This may feel like you're forcing yourself onto the recruiter, or that you are being overbearing. The truth of the matter is that there's nothing wrong with asking to follow-up with someone directly. After you get their contact information, be sure to say, "It's really nice talking to you." Try to cite something that you talked about or questions that you talked about and say like, "It was interesting that I learned this about the company." Depending on how well your conversation has gone, you can also finish it strong by asking, "When will I hear about upcoming interviews?"

The Right Action #5 - Targeted Online Search

I put this action last because if you are following the system I've outlined, you shouldn't need to search online. However, in the early stages you may be trying to locate companies in a specific city with your position. These sites can help you do that.

16 Best Websites For Online Job Search*

These are the websites that I'd suggest to find your target jobs. There are many more out there, but these are enough for you to start with. Remember, stay focused.

- **Indeed.com** - aggregates job postings from multiple websites
- **Monster.com** - large American job posting site
- **Careerbuilder.com** - large American job posting site
- **LinkedIn** - many jobs are posted here
- **TheLadders.com** - six figure and higher salary jobs
- **CollegeRecruiter.com** - enter level jobs
- **Simplyhired.com** - aggregates job postings from multiple websites
- **Oodle.com** - online job marketplace
- **TweetMyJobs.com** - aggregates jobs posted on twitter
- **Internships.com** - internships
- **Internsushi.com** - internships
- **Internmatch.com** - internships
- **Experience.com** - job site focused on college students and recent grads
- **Idealist.org** - non-profit jobs (no H-1B cap)
- **USAjobs.gov** - government jobs (no H-1B cap)

- **myvisajobs.com** - companies that have sponsored H-1B visas

*these are in no specific order of usefulness

Questions and Actions

How can I find good mentors? How did you find your mentors?
I found my best mentor at college; she was one professor that I actually liked. I really respected her and found that we have a similar outlook on life. I could see that she really cares about her students, and so had no difficulty fostering that mentor relationship. I made sure to stay connected with her, and continue to offer my help as I am able, in exchange for the assistance and guidance she has provided.

If there is someone I admire and respect, with skills that I wish to emulate, I will go out of my way to meet them. I will end up at events that they are attending or directly ask if I can take them out for coffee or lunch.

I don't have confidence in my networking skills, any suggestions how I can improve them?
Again we revisit the subject of overcoming fears and taking the more difficult path. You must build up the courage to start conversations with complete strangers. Focus on your end goal, stay positive and go to as many useful networking events as you can. The more you practice the easier it become to actually start conversations and build relationships with people. The next chapter will give you some more tips on how to get over your fears.

During networking events I collect many business cards but I have difficulty remembering the people. What should I do?
We will cover this in small talk chapter, but I will say now that when you first meet someone, the flustered, anxious feelings often make it difficult to remember details or names. If you can reduce your stress

and nervousness about such conversations, you will find that your remember names and bits of the conversations much more easily.

This trick is also useful: connect your new contact to someone you already know with the same name or a similar name, or perhaps make word connections like "Short-Sharon." Bring a pen with you and write down notes on the person's business card immediately after you're done speaking with them.

Another technique involves immediately helping that person. If you can connect them to someone else, give them information or promote something they are doing on your social media, do it while you're talking to the person. If you actually take action during a conversation and follow through with your promise immediately, you'll get a great reaction. You also will have strengthened your own memory of that new contact.

How can I increase the response rate from people I'm contacting (especially the ones in my immediate network)?

You have to help people. If you e-mail someone and say, "Hey, I'm trying to get connected to this person. Can you connect me?" It isn't likely that you get a response. The harsh reality is that people are busy with their own problems, and are usually not that concerned about your career. Try sharing a useful article with them, a free webinar, or writing them a recommendation on LinkedIn. That's always a good way to start a beneficial conversation.

Of course, when e-mail doesn't provide results I suggest picking up the phone. If you can get someone on the phone, they will be more apt to help you.

Personal Challenge

Cold-call three companies and ask for an informational interview (1 day)

Select three of your target companies. Call them and ask for an informational interview. You can call the main number on their website, and speak to whomever answers, or ask for Human resources, as they can usually help arrange the interviews. Get over your fears and don't take 'no' for an answer!

Chapter 5 - Rejection Therapy

"Fears are educated into us, and can, if we wish, be educated out."
– *Karl Menninger*

Michael Went Down to Georgia

"Who the heck am I going to be friends with here?" I thought to myself, looking around the crowded bar and then back down at my glass. I was fresh out of college and had just moved to southern Georgia. For a New England Yankee like myself, it felt like a completely different country—not to mention the fact that I didn't know a single person in the state. I was a chemical engineer and somewhat of an introvert, so I had never really been good at meeting people outside of the social network I had formed in college. On this particular night though, I had built up the courage to go to a bar full of complete strangers. Still, as I sat at the bar I could feel the paralyzing fear begin to set in. I knew that if I didn't act soon, I would be frozen. I needed to approach new people and make new friends in Georgia, otherwise my life there would be extremely boring and isolated. Despite knowing this, it was a new experience for me and **I WAS SCARED!**

Have you had the sort of experience in which everyone seems to know each other, and *you* are an "outsider"? That was me. I felt COMPLETELY out-of-place. The longer I sat there, the more I began to question myself:

"What if they make fun of me for being here alone?"

"What if they don't want to talk to me?"

"What if they laugh at me?"

I almost **paralyzed myself** with the "What if..." questions, but finally snapped out of it and focused on the goal at hand.

I knew I had two options:

1) Get over my fears, talk to people I didn't know and make new friends

or…

2) Stay scared, don't talk to anyone and live a boring, waste of a life

As you might have guessed, I went with **option 1**.

Imagining that I was probably going to get rejected, I made one more decision. If it had to happen, I thought I may as well be rejected by the best-looking girl in the bar. I spotted a pretty girl, and before I could think, I walked straight up to her and said, "Hi there. I just moved here from Bah-ston. What else is there to do around here that's fun?"

She looked me straight in the eye and squealed,

"I LOVE your accent!!! Why did you move here? What are you doing?"

She then proceeded to introduce me to EVERYONE at the bar. All of the sudden I didn't feel so alone, or so foolish.

"Is it really that easy?" I thought to myself. "Is everyone this nice?"

That moment was a turning point in my life. It was the moment that I realized that most people are open to talking to strangers. Even if they aren't, being rejected isn't that bad. There are always more people to talk to. You can also remember that rejection can be a distraction from one's original goal. Rather than become defensive and hurt, you must adopt a "who cares" attitude, and stay focused. Your goals should override the opinions of others. Also realize that you have done something incredible. Moving to a new country where you don't know anyone is **extremely brave.** I applaud any international student who has the confidence to do this. But of course, there is always room to grow and challenge yourself. I encourage you to continue to build that confidence so you can grow both personally and professionally.

Life is a continual learning experience and because of that, I've consistently challenged myself. I have continued to build my confidence when approaching strangers and making small talk. It has helped me grow personally and professionally, and allowed me to found my companies.

Fear Paralysis

You see a beautiful person across the bar from you.

"That's The One," you think to yourself. In an instant, you see your entire life play out in front of your eyes: a happy marriage, a comfortable house, a family. Your heart flutters as you start to walk across the bar towards the person. Everything is rainbows and sunshine...until you hear the flood of limiting thoughts:

"What if she say no?"

"What if he doesn't like me!?"

"What if he or she is already taken?"

Just as quickly as you fell for the person, you convince yourself that it's better to sit back down than be rejected. You cheer yourself up by thinking that there are always more people to meet, more chances like these.

Guess what? That might have been your only chance. Everyone suffers from the fear of rejection, and it's extremely challenging to overcome. But allowing it to control your actions can have painful consequences, both in the dating and the business world. Missing that one connection that would have landed you a job, made a sale, or formed a partnership is not so different from missing that one connection with a potential romantic partner. In the end, overcoming this fear will help you grow as an individual, improve your chance at happiness and separate you from the general population.

Three Tips To Overcoming Your Biggest Fears

1. Make it impossible not to follow-through

This is a trick I've used many times, with continue success. It simply means that you have to make it hard to not complete your set task. For example, you might have a friend drop you off at an event alone, and with no way of getting home. The friend will then return only when the event is over. Creating a situation like this forces you to take action. If you don't have a means of escape, you will find it easier to act. You can also use tip #3 in these situations.

You can get really creative with this tip, so take time to think about how you can put yourself in situations where you have to follow through.

2. Get others to hold you accountable

Everyone has fears. Team up. Find a friend that wants to overcome their fears as much as you. When you're at an event, hold each other accountable for the number of people you talk to. Meet periodically throughout the event and discuss your progress. If someone is behind, help them enter a conversation and start talking.

3. Act when the adrenaline is high

"Limiting thoughts" are those that go through your head when you are nervous, and that can keep you from taking action. Sadly, these limiting thoughts stop people from achieving amazing things. I'm giving you permission, in situations like these, to stop listening to those thoughts. Don't listen to them. Take action when they start (or before they even begin), when you're scared and the adrenaline is high. Use it to your advantage.

As soon as you start getting nervous, THAT IS WHEN YOU ACT.

Questions & Actions

I'm ready to go talk to go talk to Americans! How can I improve my English really quickly?

You can actually improve your language skills dramatically in about a month if you use Pareto's 80/20 rule. You need to prioritize what you are learning and eliminate the waste. I won't tell you which language school or teachers are the best, but the best system to learn a language is based on three elements in this order...

- **Effectiveness (Priority)** - Study the most practical material first: the material that will allow you to easily converse with Americans. Learn the twenty percent of words that you will use eighty percent of the time.

- **Adherence (Interest) -** Repeatedly studying material you enjoy using same exact method. Studying will seem monotonous at times, which is why it's so important to be engaged in what you're studying. Can study the material every day until you become fluent? If not, you need to make a change.

- **Efficiency (Process) -** Does the method you're using give you the best results in the shortest period of time? If the answer is no, you need to improve your method.

The 100 Most Common Spoken Words in English

1. a, an	52. on
2. after	53. one
3. again	54. only
4. all	55. or
5. almost	56. other
6. also	57. our
7. always	58. out

8. and	59. over
9. because	60. people
10. before	61. place
11. big	62. please
12. but	63. same
13. (I) can	64. (I) see
14. (I) come	65. she
15. either/or	66. so
16. (I) find	67. some
17. first	68. sometimes
18. for	69. still
19. friend	70. such
20. from	71. (I) tell
21. (I) go	72. thank you
22. good	73. that
23. goodbye	74. the
24. happy	75. their
25. (I) have	76. them
26. he	77. then
27. hello	78. there is
28. here	79. they
29. how	80. thing
30. I	81. (I) think
31. (I) am	82. this
32. if	83. time
33. in	84. to
34. (I) know	85. under
35. last	86. up
36. (I) like	87. us

37. little	88. (I) use
38. (I) love	89. very
39. (I) make	90. we
40. many	91. what
41. one	92. when
42. more	93. where
43. most	94. which
44. much	95. who
45. my	96. why
46. new	97. with
47. no	98. yes
48. not	99. you
49. now	100. your
50. of	
51. often	

The vocabulary you learn beyond the most common 100-500 words should be dictated by the subjects that you are most interested in. Ask yourself: "What do I currently spend a lot of time doing?" Those activities are probably a good place to start your search for useful new vocabulary. [1]

Personal Challenge
Get Rejected Two Times (1 Day)

This challenge is to help you overcome your fear of rejection. I want you to purposely get rejected two times. Ask someone you have never met before for their phone number. Ask your friend to give you $1000. Call a company and ask directly for a job. Whatever it is, make sure you get rejected.

When you do this on purpose, you will begin to think of it as a game and not "the end of the world." Your goal is to be rejected twice; if you don't hit that goal, you need to keep trying. Once you're done, this challenge will have put you on the path towards a new mentality. You will realize that rejection is a part of life, and not as scary as you once thought.

Personally I've tried challenges like: lying down in a crowded mall, asking random people immediately for their phone numbers, and asking for a raise when I didn't deserve one. These challenges helped me realize that being rejected does not destroy me as a person (which is amazing, because I have been rejected *many, many times*).

So go forth, and seek out rejection! It will help you grow as an individual.

Tools & Tricks

Consider Culture (www.sdendyconsiderculture.com) - The best language instructor I know. Go to her site and get in touch with her if you want to learn English faster.

Rejection Therapy (www.rejectiontherapy.com) - Website describing the personal experiment with some great tips.

LifeHacker (www.lifehacker.com) - Blog featuring cool personal experiments as well as tips and tricks to improving your personal efficiency.

BusinessEnglishPod (www.businessenglishpod.com/) - One of the best websites and mobile apps to learn business English and idioms that you will hear in every day conversation.

Chapter 6 - Be Seen as an Expert in Your Field

"An expert is a person who has made all the mistakes that can be made in a very narrow field."
-Niels Bohr, Danish physicist and Nobel Prize winner

From Who? To Guru

There I was standing in front of 105 Northeastern international students, ready to teach them how to overcome their fears and make small talk. Some "what if" questions started bubbling up into my head, but I pushed them aside as I have trained myself to do.

Adrenaline pumped into my veins as I was being introduced, and a sense or nervous excitement began to grow. I was not getting this feeling because of the number of students; I had spoken in front of much larger numbers before. Rather, I was speaking on a subject matter that I had not been deemed an "expert" in.

At the time, I had not yet been published, major news sources didn't quote me and few people knew who I was (especially the students). No one had any idea who I was, nor why I was teaching this class. One of the first questions asked was,

"What is your background?"

I could have stumbled over an answer, tried to explain why I didn't need years of experience to teach them this skill and insisted that they just 'trust me.' In short, I could have waited for their stamp of approval before continuing on with my class. Instead, I brushed it off as if my background was perfectly suited to teach them. A globe-trotting chemical-engineer-turned-entrepreneur is the perfect combination of skills to teach American culture and interpersonal relations, right? Intrigued by my journey and background the students continued to listen.

While I personally knew that I had not been teaching this class for thirty years (or even one year), I believed in myself and my ability to teach others. I knew that all of my life experiences had molded me into the perfect teacher of this subject. There was never a doubt in my mind that I was the best person to be helping those students.

That attitude and my passion for the topic showed throughout the class and the students' questions of "who are you" and "why should I believe you"... disappeared. I had instantly becoming an expert in their minds.

The class ended and I knew everyone sitting there had more confidence and a new way to approach to their lives. I knew I had helped every single person in that room. I felt a great sense of accomplishment, ready to teach students at another school. Ready to teach anyone "The Art of Small Talk"...because I was the expert.

Really? An Expert?

Whenever I tell people they can be an expert, they look at me in bewilderment. Most people don't believe that they can be an 'expert,' but it is this exact mindset that stops them from being great.

An expert is someone that knows more on a topic than 95% of the general population. That's it.

You don't need to be the smartest person in the world, have a degree from Harvard or be praised by large media sources. But how do you avoid the initial self-doubt? How do you take action and BELIEVE in your own expertise?

For me, I needed a wake-up call. It was necessary that someone tell me that I would never get an announcement in the New York Times saying, "Here is Michael Miller: Cross-culture and international career development EXPERT." If I waited for that day, I would be waiting (and wasting) my entire life.

This blew my mind. I suddenly realized I *was* waiting to be dubbed an expert and it was slowing me down. Don't make this mistake. You can be an expert as soon as you recognize your own potential.

There are the two things needed to become an expert: passion and specificity. By following your career blueprint, you have already pinpointed what you are passionate about, and are pursuing it in a specific, organized manner. In my case, it's a lot easier to be an expert in international career development in America than it is to be a "cross-cultural expert." The same small distinctions will apply to whatever dream you are chasing.

Becoming the Guru

Many people don't know where to begin when I tell them to "become an expert." Let me show you a variety of ways you can quickly and actively become an expert in your field.

Start a Blog

I **strongly** suggest that you start a blog. It will not only help you become an expert but it will help you narrow your field. You will write about things you enjoy and over time you'll notice patterns and topics that you find easier to write about.

Speak Publicly

If you speak publicly at conferences, events, schools or businesses, it will build your reputation as an expert. Try to get whatever speaking gigs you can because the more you practice, the more confident you will become. Also, whenever you speak make sure to record it and put it on your YouTube channel. Future employers will love seeing "evidence" of your expertise.

Get on Twitter

There are millions of people on twitter looking for experts. You can be that expert. Get an account and start posting useful tips, articles and blog posts. Follow people in your specific industry and show them that you are worth following. Tweet @ them and start a conversation. No matter what industry you are in, twitter will eventually have a positive impact on your career.

Be Active in LinkedIn Groups
I've told you to join 52 LinkedIn groups that have to do with your specific goal. Now it's time to show the people in those groups that you exist. Post useful content to them and partake in discussions happening in the groups. Try to show that you are innovative and have your own original thoughts.

Get Certifications
Many different majors or industries have certifications you can get to show your expertise. For instance, if you are in the accounting field, you can get your CPA (Certified Public Accountant) accreditation. In many engineering fields, you can get a FE (Fundamentals of Engineering) accreditation. If you get certifications like these, there are many companies that will be interested in hiring you.

Pro Bono Projects
Ask companies if there are any projects you can do for them pro bono (for no pay). Of course, you need to make sure this work is legal first. Then you could conduct a research study or write a guest blog post, etc. The tangible results from these projects can bolster your résumé.

Volunteering
You can also volunteer for professional organizations or events. It's a great way to get experience with a specific industry and add to your résumé.

Take Free Online Courses
There are many websites where anyone in the world can now take free online courses, including Edx.org, Coursera.org, Udemy.com,

Creativelive.com, Skillshare.com, etc. There are courses on business, science, art, psychology, finance...everything. Find something relevant to your specific goal.

Find Role Models
You can emulate these role models and they can also mentor you. I have a couple of mentors who helped me get over the initial thought that I couldn't be an expert. Without this support I would not be where I am now.

Questions & Actions

Why is twitter important?
Besides the obvious personal network benefits, it's one of the easiest way to get in touch with companies and high powered people. Want an informational interview? Try tweeting at a company or person. I also feel that it's important to keep up with technology trends to ensure that you are on the cutting edge of innovation.

What if there's absolutely no way I would be considered an expert in my field without ten years of experience?
First, that doesn't seem like a very innovative field to me. Second, I would strongly question that judgment. Rules are meant to be broken and you should be the one trying to break them. Recently, a ten year old *kid* graduated from the University of Southern Alabama, while an eight-year old became "Microsoft Certified Technology Specialist." [1][2] Don't let limiting thoughts hold you back from greatness.

Personal Challenge

Start A Blog (1 Day)

Starting a blog will take five minutes. Writing your first post should only take an hour or two. Soon you'll be building content and creating a portfolio to support your status as an expert. So how do you start one?

Go to Wordpress.com and sign up. Choose a web address that is recognizable and memorable (not too complicated). Now you have a means to publish on the internet! Time to write your first post...

Boom. Step 1 to becoming an expert in your field is complete.

Later you can link to this blog on your résumé, your LinkedIn profile, Twitter, Facebook, etc. All you have to do is write about one post per week. This one post is enough to show your expertise.

If you really don't enjoy writing, there are other options. You could always create videos, for example. As long as it's informational and helps people, it will solidify your role as an expert.

Once you've started, it is easy to promote your posts to socially influential contacts or successful people in your industry. Eventually someone will take notice and direct others to your blog. You might get lucky and someone in the media might want your opinion on a topic.

Tools & Tricks

Drafting Technique - To get more people to visit your blog, you can use a technique called 'drafting,' which was created by Derek Halpern of Social Triggers.com. [3]

How does 'drafting' work?

When a race car drafts (stays really close) behind another race car, it begins to gain speed. The air is broken by the first car thereby allowing the second car to more easily maintain and gain speed. You are going to do the same thing with your blog posts.

Basically, you choose a hot news story that is related to your expertise. Then you write a blog on that same topic with a different spin to it. You could have some different data than the original author, or an opposing opinion. Whatever you choose, make sure that you then tweet, send or share it with the original author. More often than not, they will give a reaction or defend their point. This will get you more exposure and show your inventive thought-process. Who knows, you might even attract thousands of people that want to hear more of your opinions.

Clarity.fm - A web service that makes it easy for anyone to get or give advice. You can create a profile to show off your expertise and actually even charge people for advice.

Elance (www.elance.com) - A website where you can register as a "freelancer" or consultant for almost any field. You can try to land consulting jobs from people and companies all over the world.

Odesk (www.odesk.com) - A website similar to Elance, where you can register as a "freelancer" or consultant for almost any field. I personally use Odesk quite often to outsource simple tasks.

Chapter 7 - Résumé Perfection

One important key to success is self-confidence. An important key to self-confidence is preparation. - *Arthur Ashe*

Blood Type What?

I had just begun looking through my slew of about 80 internship applications for Culture Adapt. Unfortunately, I always dread this process because of the sheer number of BAD applications I get.

For example, most of the applicants had a résumé that didn't show any experience that I was looking for, and those who did had buried it in a confusing mess of bolded and italicized words. I kept thinking to myself, "I don't care where you go to school or what your GPA is. I don't care what your major is. Just show me the skill I asked for in the job posting!"

Bad résumé after bad résumé after bad résumé. At last, I came to a resume that shocked me. It looked like this:

"Maybe it's normal to show your blood type and social picture in their home country?" I thought to myself. As I scanned the document, I was astounded to see the worst résumé I had ever encountered. The applicant had put absolutely no effort into Americanizing it, and because of this I was unable to see her as a serious candidate.

I moved on, still looking for the one specific skill set I needed. In the end, I only found it in about five résumés. I began to read the cover letters. Once again, I was crestfallen. Every applicant had given me nearly identical cover letters, which essentially broke down to the plea:

"I love different cultures. I'd love to work at your company. Can you help me?"

Now, I love helping people. When someone merely asks for a 'hand out,' with no suggestion of what they could do in return, it completely turns me off. Me, and every other employer are looking for new employees. We aren't looking to hand someone a job because he likes "the idea" of working for us. We want a someone capable of contributing to our goals in big ways.

In the end I decided to go with a student I met at an event and had a conversation with.

The Lesson

This example is a little extreme, but it will hopefully show you how important it is to adapt your resume to American standards. Every country has slightly different standards and expectations for résumés. If you do not meet them, your résumé will be thrown out. Running the company I do, I receive résumés from around the world. If they do not meet the standards, I don't bother to look any further. I guarantee you that almost every American company does the same.

Before and After

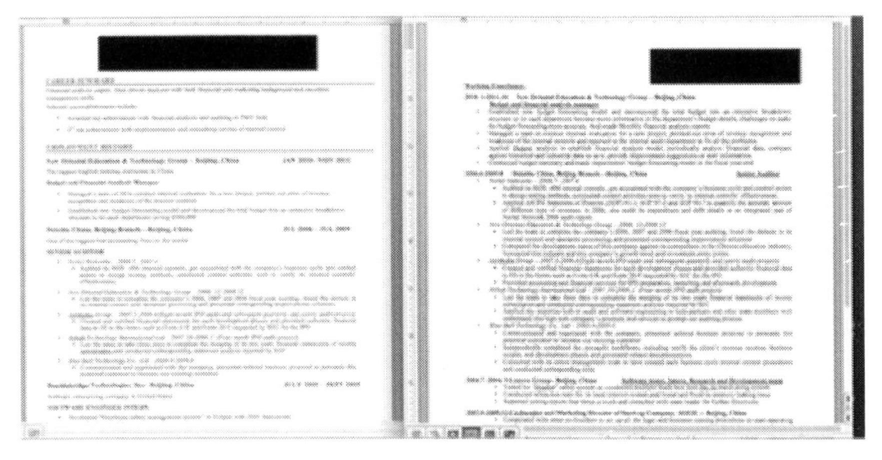

As I mentioned earlier in the book, once you have edited your résumé and perfected it, you shouldn't have to touch it again. This picture above shows one of my student's résumés before (right) using my tips and template and after (left) perfecting it. You can see just glancing at the different resumes that the left one is much easier to read and has a more Americanized format. The dates are formatted differently, the structure is different and the information is different. You have to make sure that you update your résumé to not only fit American standards, but also to catch the hiring manager's eyes.

Let's take a closer look at some of the updates that we made to this résumé and show how it presents this person in the best possible way. The first thing we did was change the format. Right away you can see that it is more streamlined, cleaner, and much easier to read. The reader can clearly see where each section begins and ends.

We also added a career summary, so right off the bat the reader can see the many ways in which this person's experience relates to the position that they are applying for.

When we get to the section where they start describing their work experience, it is difficult to tell at a glance where one job ends and the other one begins. This is because the spacing is too little in between lines and because they have **too much information**.

A hiring manager would take a quick glance at the old résumé and throw it out. There was a lot of great information on it, but the manager would assume that the applicant is not a top candidate because of the format.

American Résumé Tips

Make sure it fits on one page
It doesn't need to be two pages unless you have an advanced degree or 10+ years of experience and simply cannot fit everything on one page. Americans like résumés to be concise and to the point, as they are trained to make quick assessments.

Select Format Which Follows Your Qualifications
No matter what position you are trying to get, you have to realize what is most important to your potential employer. Is it where you went to school and your degree? Or the work experience you have? Make sure you format your résumé correctly. In this case, it can be helpful to ask your mentors for help as they likely have more experience.

No Underlining
You should avoid underlining because it makes it harder to read. Only use bold headings, as to make the resume as clear and easy to read as possible.

No pictures, age, sex or personal information
You should not have any personal information other than your contact information. Again this is a cultural thing but if you put other items on the resume then there is a greater chance that it will be dismissed.

Choose headings that spark a reader's' interest
Think about what would spark the interest of someone if they are just glancing at a resume.

Don't list ALL the boring day-to-day stuff
Employers don't really care about your day-to-day tasks. They understand that everyone has normal work that they have had to do, but ultimately, that's not what separates you from the pack. Keep this to a minimum. Instead, provide specifically striking achievements, personal development, etc.

Use measurable results to highlight achievements
You want to cite metrics and numbers that give the scale of your projects and experiences. Employers want to see measurable results because they want proof that you can help them solve their problems. If you have really strong results, that can separate your resume from every other one.

Use action words
Throughout your résumé, you want to use action words like 'accomplished,' 'saved,' 'generated,' 'created,' 'developed,' etc. Use these words to form your bullet points or sentences.

Don't use an objective sentence
Your stated 'Objectives' used to be an important part of a résumé. It is now seen as out-dated and superfluous. Remember, it's how you can help an employer, not how they can help you.

Use the 80/20 rule
It's a great rule for everything! Use the 80/20 rule to minimize the information on your résumé. Twenty percent of the information is going to lead to eighty percent of your interviews, so make sure you figure out what that twenty percent is. What are the skills and experiences that make you the perfect candidate?

Don't use résumé templates from Microsoft Word
So many people simply plug in their personal information in the appropriate places on a résumé templates found in Microsoft Word. Hiring managers have seen these templates hundreds (if not *thousands*) of time. Such presentation certainly won't help you stand out from the competition. Even worse, it may lead hiring manager to conclude that you lack creativity, imagination or individual thought. I would suggest using my résumé template or to look online for sample résumés that you can build on and customize.

Avoid carelessness
Hiring managers will tell you that the number one reason your résumé ended up in the trash can was because of your minor spelling errors, grammar mistakes and typos. It is crucial that you read your résumé carefully…then reread it…and then have someone else proofread it for you. Often a fresh pair of eyes can catch mistakes that maybe you have overlooked. This five-minute editing process could be the difference between getting the interview or not, so don't skip it!

Appropriate e-mail address
Another thing that will get your résumé thrown in the trash can is if you have an inappropriate kind of e-mail address in your contact information. Make sure that you use a professional e-mail address (which means one with both your first and last name, or first initial and last name).

Use one font
Many people use too many fonts in their resume and overwhelm the reader. One is sufficient to present a clear, concise and organized look.

Use appropriate spacing

Too much white space at the top of a résumé can be unappealing. Too little space in the middle can make it confusing and hard to read. Keep an even balance.

My Résumé

Michael Miller

Address, City, State Zip • (xxx) xxx-xxxx • email@gmail.com

CAREER SUMMARY

Continuous Improvement specialist with exceptional interpersonal skills. An expert in both Lean Manufacturing and Six Sigma. Outstanding trainer with strong mentoring capabilities. Has superb project management skills and seeks to promote continuous improvement within your organization. Selected accomplishments include:

- Drove continuous improvement movement at two facilities, one being the most complex and the other being the largest in all of Dean Foods, which led to 2 million dollars in annual savings from 2010 projects alone.
- Drove OEE improve project that lead to an 11% overall OEE improvement which allowed the facility to condense from 14 down to 11 production lines.
- Designed and implemented Lean Manufacturing Program in Suzhou, China which led to a 4.1% overall yield improvement and savings of $250,000/year.

EMPLOYMENT HISTORY

Dean Foods- Franklin and Lynn, MA **APRIL 2010– PRESENT**
12 billion dollar dairy company with 100 plants across the US and Europe.

CONTINUOUS IMPROVEMENT MANAGER

- Lead network optimization team between two Garelick Farms (Franklin and Lynn) plants that lead to a net savings of ~$200,000/year.
- Participate jointly with other CI Managers in corporate process improvement events at various manufacturing plants.
- Responsible for coaching, functional training, communications, base lining, and identifying and transferring best practices externally and internally.

Hollingsworth & Vose– East Walpole, MA **JUNE 2009 – APRIL 2010**
400 million dollar with manufacturing facilities in Europe, Asia, and North America.

PROCESS ENGINEER at West Groton Facility

- Stand-in production supervisor for 30+ employees.
- Facilitated business and manufacturing Kaizen events including: Improve customer service and on-time-delivery by 2%, improve supply chain and decrease inventory by $200,000, and improve grade start times by 5 minutes.
- Completed Six Sigma project on ultrasonic bonding line that improved yield by 2% saving over $100,000/year.
- Mentored Black Belts, Green Belts and coached Kaizen facilitators.

ASSOCIATE DEVELOPMENT PROGRAM **JUNE 2007 – MAY 2009**
Selected to be in 2-year leadership development program to accelerate learning curve and career development.

- Completed four 6-month rotations at three US facilities and one international. (East Walpole, MA; Hawkinsville, GA; Floyd, VA; Suzhou, China)
- Total process improvement project savings during program- $367,000/year

EDUCATION

B.S., Chemical Engineering

Worcester Polytechnic Institute

CONTINUING EDUCATION

- **Certified Lean Agent by Six Sigma.US**
- MassMEP Lean 101- Principles of Lean
- Kaizen Facilitator by FinTek
- **Certified Six Sigma Black Belt by SixSigma.US**
- Dale Carnegie High Impact Presentations
- AMA Communication and Interpersonal Skills

TECHNICAL PROFICIENCIES

- Minitab 15 Statistical Software, Microsoft Office Suite, Visio, Oracle, MathCAD and AutoCAD

This is my résumé. With this résumé, I got into the leadership development program, and obtained my manager position at the Fortune 500 Company.

I include the following sections: career summary, employment history, education, continuing education, and technical proficiencies. You'll notice under my education I didn't list my graduation date. I did this because I knew I was trying to get a position that required ten years of experience and didn't want a hiring manager to guess my age.

I personally believe that for many managerial positions, it doesn't matter how much experience you have. Instead, your ability to learn, innovate and your interpersonal skills should determine your suitability for the position. You'll notice once you get into an interview situation, people will be less concerned about the year you graduated and more concerned about how you can help them. I imagine that omitting that date from my résumé helped me get the interview and the job.

Michael Miller

Address • XXX.XXX.XXXX • example@gmail.com

CAREER SUMMARY

Continuous Improvement specialist with exceptional interpersonal skills. An expert in both Lean Manufacturing and Six Sigma. Outstanding trainer with strong mentoring capabilities. Has superb project management skills and seeks to promote continuous improvement within your organization. Selected accomplishments include:

- Drove continuous improvement movement at two facilities, one being the most complex and the other being the largest in all of Dean Foods, which led to 2 million dollars in annual savings from 2010 projects alone.
- Drove OEE improve project that lead to an 11% overall OEE improvement which allowed the facility to condense from 14 down to 11 production lines.
- Designed and implemented Lean Manufacturing Program in Suzhou, China which led to a 4.1% overall yield improvement and savings of $250,000/year.

EMPLOYMENT HISTORY

Dean Foods- Franklin and Lynn, MA **APRIL 2010– PRESENT**

12 billion dollar dairy company with 100 plants across the US and Europe.

CONTINUOUS IMPROVEMENT MANAGER

- Lead network optimization team between two Garelick Farms (Franklin and Lynn) plants that lead to a net savings of ~$200,000/year.
- Participate jointly with other CI Managers in corporate process improvement events at various manufacturing plants.
- Responsible for coaching, functional training, communications, base lining, and identifying and transferring best practices externally and internally.

Hollingsworth & Vose– East Walpole, MA **JUNE 2009 – APRIL 2010**

400 million dollar with manufacturing facilities in Europe, Asia, and North America.

PROCESS ENGINEER at West Groton Facility

The graduation date trick was important for my position, but the career summary is the most important part of your résumé. Recruiters and hiring managers see hundreds of résumés a week, so you have to catch their attention immediately. The career summary offers a chance to catch their attention, so start your résumé with it.

The career summary gives any reader a quick glimpse at who you are, why you are unique, and why you might be valuable than others. It begins with two or three short, descriptive sentences about your specialties. These sentences should relate to the characteristics on your career blueprint for your dream position.

After your summary, list the top three accomplishments throughout your career. These should impress and show your expertise. These may take some time for you to formulate, but the effort will be worth it.

When I look at résumés, I typically don't need to look anywhere beyond the accomplishments. In this small section I know

I'll find a way to measure what this person has done, what characteristics they find important and if they can help me.

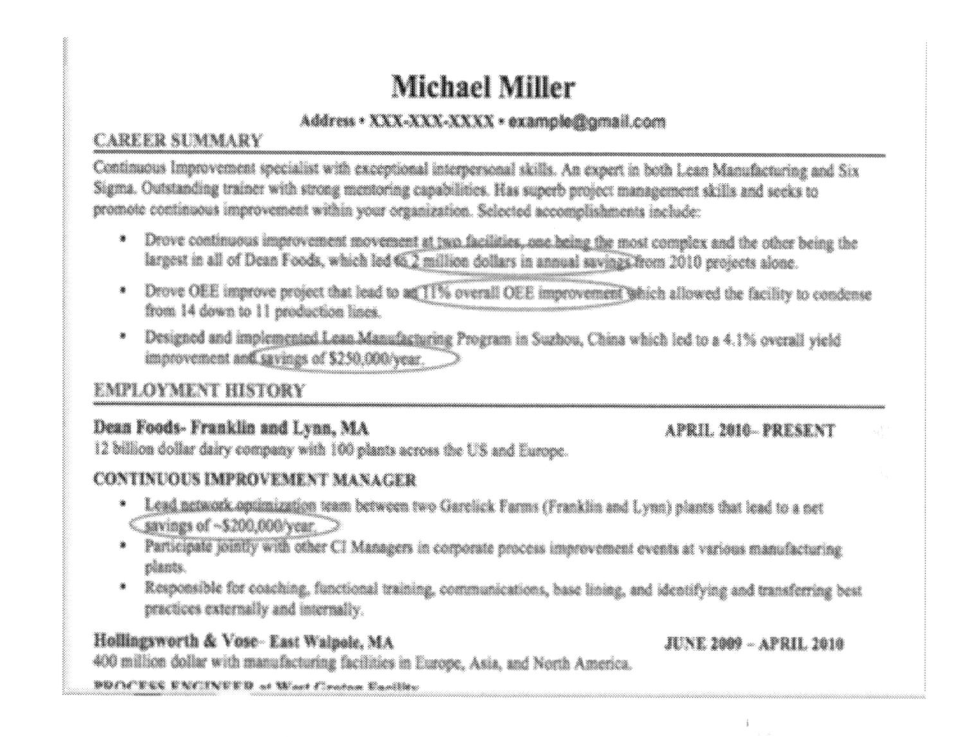

Michael Miller

Address • XXX-XXX-XXXX • example@gmail.com

CAREER SUMMARY

Continuous Improvement specialist with exceptional interpersonal skills. An expert in both Lean Manufacturing and Six Sigma. Outstanding trainer with strong mentoring capabilities. Has superb project management skills and seeks to promote continuous improvement within your organization. Selected accomplishments include:

- Drove continuous improvement movement at two facilities, one being the most complex and the other being the largest in all of Dean Foods, which led to 2 million dollars in annual savings from 2010 projects alone.
- Drove OEE improve project that lead to an 11% overall OEE improvement which allowed the facility to condense from 14 down to 11 production lines.
- Designed and implemented Lean Manufacturing Program in Suzhou, China which led to a 4.1% overall yield improvement and savings of $250,000/year.

EMPLOYMENT HISTORY

Dean Foods- Franklin and Lynn, MA **APRIL 2010– PRESENT**

12 billion dollar dairy company with 100 plants across the US and Europe.

CONTINUOUS IMPROVEMENT MANAGER

- Lead network optimization team between two Garelick Farms (Franklin and Lynn) plants that lead to a net savings of ~$200,000/year.
- Participate jointly with other CI Managers in corporate process improvement events at various manufacturing plants.
- Responsible for coaching, functional training, communications, base lining, and identifying and transferring best practices externally and internally.

Hollingsworth & Vose- East Walpole, MA **JUNE 2009 – APRIL 2010**

400 million dollar with manufacturing facilities in Europe, Asia, and North America.

Showing measurable results is also essential to do in a résumé. Employers don't care if you worked on 'this client,' or contributed for three months to 'this project.' Their main concern is your ability to make an impact. Companies run on money, so if you can show them that you can help save or make them money, they will be interested.

Look at my personal results circled in the picture above. First you see "2 million dollars in annual savings." If that doesn't catch someone's attention then I don't know what will. The next result of "11% OEE" describes a process improvement project. I have listed it as it would be detailed in the industry (which shows my experience). The following two results are "savings of $250,000/year" and "savings of $200,000/year." The dollar signs will always be eye-catching, because companies LOVE saving money!

If you haven't completed any projects with monetary results, then it's important to figure out what other metrics you can use that will still be impressive. Some examples include customers satisfaction increase, new customers acquired, website visitor growth, hours taught, etc. You could even go back to some projects you've done in school or show how well your blog is doing. If a lot of people are reading your blog or you got mentioned in a major media source, that is a powerful, more quantifiable addition.

It's okay to list your position responsibilities, because this is a great place to plug in keywords. If you do that, though, make sure that you avoid phrases like "duties included" or "responsible for." These hackneyed phrases can better replaced with powerful action verbs like 'created,' 'developed,' 'managed,' and 'led.'

Résumé Keywords

The number one mistake that people make is not using keywords on the text of their résumé.

More and more companies are starting to use resume database software or applicant tracking systems (ATS). Hiring managers will type in a few keywords related to the position that they are hiring for and resumes with those keywords on them will show up. The systems work on a percentage basis, so if your résumé doesn't hit the required percentage of matching keywords, it will never reach the hiring manager's screen.

It is really important to carefully read the job description and incorporate keywords throughout the text of your résumé. At the same time you want to make sure you do this naturally. For example, you don't want to take an entire sentence word for word from the job description and wedge it into your résumé. It will look out of place and ridiculous. Instead, you want to look for keywords like job titles, specific skills that they are asking for, certifications they may want, and things like industry acronyms. Then find places on your résumé to naturally insert those keywords.

You can use these keywords throughout your cover letter and also make them a part of your overall personal brand. Put them on you blog, your LinkedIn profile, your social media; make sure you use those keywords all the time. Since you're becoming an expert in a specific niche, it will be useful to you.

I again want to remind you that while important, these keywords are something you don't need to worry about if you are directly connecting with the right people. Building relationships is the best way to completely bypass a company's ATS.

Questions and Actions

If I'm living outside the country should I put my foreign address?
Yes, because that's where you are and eventually the employer is going to figure that out. However, as I stated in Chapter 2, if you are flexible with your schedule and ability to travel, you should make it apparent.

If my industry is not sales or savings driven and my projects/work experience has never been monetarily based, how do I show results?
You can show how many customers or clients you've helped, how many hours you've logged, how many people or facilities you managed, etc. Just make sure that the results you show are going to impress your employer and show the value you can provide.

I still don't know what action words to use on my résumé. Any suggestions?
Using the correct action words will be important for your résumé and any other professional writing. There are hundreds of action words specific to different skill sets and industries. If you're having trouble finding more, Boston College has a great list that you can use here: http://www.bc.edu/offices/careers/skills/resumes/verbs.html

Are extra-curricular activities important?
It depends. Some employers or hiring managers like to see people that are active in their community, schools or industry. Some don't care. I would advise that you are active in extra-curricular activities to 1) grow your network 2) become more familiar with American culture 3) grow your expertise and 4) have a little bit of fun.

Be careful about adding them to your resume because you want to make sure that you are showing them your entire skill set and achievements on just one page. When I was younger and had less experience, I had my extra-curricular activities on my résumé. Once I had enough experience, I didn't see the value in it. I knew that I could discuss my interests outside of work during interviews.

What should I do if I don't have any work experience?
Think back to the ways that you can become an expert: volunteering, blogging, pro-bono projects, shadowing mentors, etc. All of these avenues allow you to get experience before ever getting your first job. If you still haven't done any of these, make sure you take action immediately, get involved and grow your expertise. You also might have to format your résumé differently by focusing on your impressive academic experience.

What should my cover letter look like?
Take a look at mine on the next page. It should be short, to the point and relatively generic. Do it once and do it right.

Michael Miller

Address Line 1
City, MA 02135
(xxx) xxx-xxx
email@gmail.com

Company
Freedom Dr.
Reston, VA 20190

February 1, 2010

Dear Hiring Manager,

Please except my application for the position of BLANK. My experience as a shift supervisor, kaizen facilitator, Six Sigma Black Belt, project manager and lean agent provide me with the knowledge that is needed to excel in this position. I would attack the challenges presented with pride, tenacity and energy thereby ensuring that we reach our goals.

At Hollingsworth and Vose, I became the first employee to obtain both their Six Sigma Black Belt and Lean Agent certifications. My process improvement and Lean projects have provided the most savings of any engineer over the last two year period. By working in five different factories over the last two years, I have learned to analyze and improve new processes quickly. This has also allowed me to help Hollingsworth and Vose globally change their culture to a lean manufacturing company. I want to provide this same type of success as a Lean Six Sigma Consultant.

I excel in my current profession not only because I possess all the problem solving and analytic skills of an engineer, but also because I have exceptional interpersonal skills. I would use these skills to provide coaching and training to employees, facilitate kaizen events, lead project teams and promote the continuous improvement culture.

I am eager to help advance the success of your company, and I would welcome the opportunity to discuss in further detail my skills and experience, and interest in working for Accenture. I look forward to hearing from you and thank you for your consideration.

Sincerely,

Michael Miller

Personal Challenge
The 15 Second Test (2 days)

Once you've edited your résumé, I want you to do the "15 second test" with five people. This is a test where you ask someone to look at your résumé for 15 seconds and take it away.

Why fifteen?

Because that is how much time a recruiting manager will take to look completely over that piece of paper. They are breezing through hundreds of resumes a week, so in fifteen seconds they have already made a judgment of whether they are interested in you or not.

Let each person look at it for fifteen seconds, take it away from them, ask them to describe you. What did they find out by quickly reading that résumé? Ask them to sum you up in one or two sentences.

You have a thought in your mind of how you are conveying yourself on your résumé, right?

By doing this test, you can easily see if you are being successful in conveying that message. If you are not, then you have to edit your résumé. Maybe the format is not as good as it should be, or perhaps your career summary stinks, or maybe your accomplishments don't seem as impressive as they really are.

You can do this quick test repeatedly to figure out if your résumé is perfect and conveying the right message.

So here are the steps again:

1. Bring your résumé to five different people
2. Let them look it over for fifteen seconds
3. Take it away
4. Ask them to describe you
5. Ask them to sum you up in a sentence or two
6. Decide if you are conveying the correct message
7. Adjust your résumé accordingly

Part 3:
Follow Through

"Networking is an essential part of building wealth." – *Armstrong Williams*

Chapter 8 - Master Networking

"See the good in people and help them." - *Gandhi*

The First Time

Jnanesh had never been to an American professional networking event outside of those held by his university. American's might find this strange; Jnanesh was confident, intelligent and driven...so what had been stopping him?

Very simply, nothing. There was nothing preventing Jnanesh from attending networking events. He simply didn't see the need, as it wasn't an important part of his country's business culture.

When I first learned this, he had been interning at my company, Socialete, for just a couple weeks. I decided to ask him to attend a networking event with me. He happily obliged, even saying how excited he was to attend his first event. Then he paused, and looked at me. "Mike," he said, "how do I start a conversation, and what do I talk about?"

At this point, we sat down and I explained to him the normality of such casual conversation, in which you walk up to anyone (regardless of age, gender, and profession) and talk casually about light topics. I told him it was extremely common in America and that he shouldn't be worried. This seemed to ease some of his nervousness. A big smile came across his face as he told me, "I can't wait for the event!"

I was happy with his open attitude towards something completely foreign to him. I had always enjoyed his company, and knew others would as well.

At last the day of the networking event arrived, and a last-minute emergency prevented me from attending. I was concerned that he would be overcome by the fear of rejection and decided to tell him a great trick I used to start conversations: pictures.

People love getting pictures taken of themselves and it normally gets conversation started. I had used this in many different situations and it always worked. I told him we could post pictures of the event on our blog and to make sure he got people's contact info so he could follow up with them and send them the pictures. I did this instruction all via text and hoped that it would give him the courage to "break the ice" and start conversations. The next came and I wondered how the event had gone for him. Would he feel uncomfortable and completely demoralized?

"Hey Michael!" I heard him call, as he walked into the office the next day. "I talked to so many people and got all their business cards! It was great!"

I was proud of him and impressed with his courage. "That's awesome!" I replied, knowing that this had been an extremely important life experience for him.

Jnanesh now works in Arizona in the management consulting industry.

Are you looking for people in the wrong places?

A while back I was mentoring a student who was trying to get a job in online marketing. He was a brilliant student, nice person and driven to get a job. There was just one problem: HE WASN'T GETTING ANY INTERVIEWS!

I was perplexed by this, and decided I needed to find out more. I set up a meeting over coffee and sat down with him.

"So let's figure out why you're failing." I said. In cases like this, it is most useful to be straightforward. He looked a little worn down when he replied, "I don't know Mike. I'm following your advice and going to networking events up to five times a week. I guess I'm just not that lucky."

I knew as soon as he used the word "lucky" that he was doing something wrong. We talked a little more and I quickly figured out the problem. He had been attending ANY networking event he could. His mindset was **quantity over quality**. He might as well of been applying online! There is such a scarce possibility that you are going to meet the right people at your dream company if you aren't specific. Without this focus, your event attendance and informational interviews provide little for you.

To remedy my student's situation, I encouraged him to think about how he could meet the people he needed to connect with. What events do they attend? How could he find those events? How could he get informational interviews with those people without ever meeting them?

When the meeting ended, I could see that his confidence was restored. I knew he was going to start seeing results.

Too many people make this same mistake

Example 1

An overseas student of mine wanted to work for a giant technology company in America. She had a great résumé, enthusiastic attitude and was ready to take on the challenge of getting a job here. To do this, she decided to plan a trip to Boston to meet company contacts and hopefully get some interviews. This tactic was at the recommendation of my online Dream Job Achiever class, in which I challenged my overseas students to get informational interviews with people at their target companies. I decided to follow up with her and find out how her preparations were going.

"I'm just going to wait until I get to America to set up meetings," she told me. "It's expensive to call from here."

"Skype is cheap and you should have MULTIPLE meetings set up **before you arrive**," I suggested. "If you wait, who knows what will happen?"

Sure enough a couple days later I got an email saying "I have multiple meetings set up with people at three of my target tech companies, and am going to be getting more."

Boom! That is how you take action (even from overseas)!

Example 2

This particular person wanted to get a job in the Marketing/IT field. At the start, he did an amazing job of meeting the right people, and was able to connect with a manager at EMC. From there, the manager internally recommended his application! Great success, but why stop there? He still had other companies to target. Surprisingly, the second time around he decided to apply online.

Why? Even after the first success, communication and networking is intimidating. It's a lot harder to meet people than it is to click "submit" online. Of course, this was not going to get him results. Luckily, as his mentor I was able to get him back on the right path, targeting individuals at companies and trying to get internally recommended.

Are you looking for people in the wrong places?

Here is an easy test that I like to do: when I arrive to a networking event I ask myself two questions.

1) Who is here that I need to meet?

2) If I don't who, why the heck am I here wasting my precious time?

Wow. How easy is that test? Before you attend an event you should know your exact goal. Is there a specific person you're trying to meet? Are multiple people from one of your dream companies going to be there? Is it an industry event with five of your dream companies attending? Once you figure those questions out, set a goal for the number of people you want to build relationships with at the event.

This goal is key! When people don't have a goal in mind, they tend to waste time talking to just one or two people the entire event. Setting a goal will force you to manage your time, and push you to meet more people.

Six Tips To Building Your Confidence

Remember, at a networking event the worst-case scenario sees you sitting silently, not speaking to anyone for fear that you'll be rejected. Here are some tips to help you build your confidence and stay focused on your goal for the event.

1. Practice
The best way to get better at networking is to practice. Practice starting conversations, approaching people or entering into new situations. Acknowledge that that fear may always exist, but it doesn't have to slow you down. I still get nervous approaching CEOs of large companies, but that doesn't stop me from starting the conversation.

2. Meditate
This may sound crazy to some of you, but it works. You'll be surprised how helpful five to ten minutes can be when you clearing your mind and accept the insignificance of most of your life encounters. Techniques and proper practice can be learned about online.

3. Read books
At the end of the book, I list a number of books that I have read over the years and found particularly useful. Education continues beyond the classroom, and the more steps you take on your own, the fast you'll grow.

4. Exercise more
When you exercise, your brain releases endorphins, adrenaline, serotonin and dopamine. These chemicals all work together to make you feel good. In addition, after exercising you will feel a sense of accomplishment and power.

5. Improve you appearance
First impressions matter. Look at your role models and how they present themselves. I've changed my appearance dramatically over the years and it garners respect. My personal favorite saying? "You can never be overdressed."

6. Improve your posture
Posture is important and something that I worked on and actually practiced. Every day I would stand with my back against a wall for two minutes. Making my heels, shoulders and the back of my head all touch it. It was extremely uncomfortable at first but paid off in the end.

The Secret to Networking

Even after building your confidence, networking will still be hard.

Why?

First, let's look at what networking really is. In a recent survey 8 out of 10 people couldn't explain networking. They could not define the concept behind it, the purpose, nor how to do it effectively. That means that if you understand this, you're better off than 80% of the general population.

So what is the big secret? What is networking?

Very simply, networking works when there is a **constant flow of useful information**. Sounds simple, right? If you have information that's useful to others and they have information that's useful to you, you are successfully networking.

It stands to reason, then that if that flow of information stops, there is no point to that network. Understanding this simple fact will set you apart from most people that network with no real goals or idea what they're doing.

Establish A Power Network

Something else you should do to improve your networking skills is to establish a power network. This power network can help you find specific networking events, connect with specific people, or push you to talk to more people at an event.

There are three types of people involved in this network.

Cornerstones - People that you rely on weekly, daily or even more often to tell you about upcoming events, go to events with you, and introduce you to other people. These are people that you rely on to help push you in the right direction.

Experts - These are people with more knowledge and experience than you, and who can guide you. They can provide the social proof that you are lacking, and the credibility that you need. In life, if you surround yourself with people that are smarter than you, by default you will become more intelligent.

Tangential Helpers - These are the people that can connect you to other individuals, groups or just help you from time to time with the expectation that you will help them in return.

You can typically find these three types of people from your network of mentors that we discussed earlier in the book. Once the network is set up, try setting up weekly upcoming event email with them and build some kind of a routine. As with all aspects of your career search, specificity is key. Defining these three types people for yourself will make your networking attempts more successful. [1]

Setting Event Goals

Events are no different from the rest of your career journey. You need to be specific to be successful. Focus on only going to networking events that will help you reach the goals on your blueprint. Set a goal for yourself on how many people you want to meet and how many relationships you want to build at the event. This will help you manage your time. It is easy to get caught up talking to one or two people for an entire networking event if you don't focus on not doing that.

So before you go to an event set three goals for yourself.

1) How many people and business cards you want to get? (I suggest at least ten for a one-hour event)

2) How many relationships and job leads you want to get?

3) How many specific people are you going to meet?

Write these goals down before the event and then judge yourself after the event. If you didn't reach your goals then you know you need to improve.

Successful Follow-Up

After you meet the right people you have to follow up properly or you can ruin the entire relationship.

Also, if you don't follow up with people they are going to have a tougher time remembering you. Without a solid connection to you, they are much less likely to help you.

Follow-up can be done via e-mail, phone call, Skype, LinkedIn or even using a video message. If you are going to send a written follow-up, I would suggest using my follow up template.

Hi (First Name),
Nice to meet you the other (day, night, event, etc.).
Sentence 1.
Sentence 2.
Sentence 3.
Regards, (or Thanks,)
Your Name
P.S. – (Anything you really want people to read)

Sentence 1- The memory
You pull something from your past conversation that he/she will remember you by.

Options:
It was great speaking with you about ________. It really interests me.
I was thinking about our discussion the other day and...
I wanted to follow up with the information I told you about...

Sentence 2- The help sentence
How you can help them or why you can help them.

My background in X, Y could help you with _________ because...
I did a little research online and found that...
I looked into this and found...
Here is the contact info of the person I said I'd connect you to....
Here's an interesting article I thought you would like...

Sentence 3 - The ask
Asking them to help you in some way.

I'd love to meet up for a quick coffee and discuss this further with you. When do you have some time?
I'd love to discuss this further with you. When do you have time for a quick phone call?
I'll be in Boston on xx/xx. Is there a chance we could meet up for a little bit?

P.S. – Additional important info.
Most people read whatever is written in the postscript, even if they don't read the rest of your e-mail.

Questions & Actions

How can I constantly make the flow of useful information?
If you are attending an industry event, knowing new, interesting or relevant industry information will be useful. Also knowledge of any upcoming events in your industry can be really valuable information to share. If you're at an industry or social event, you can provide entertaining stories or suggest interesting new experiences for someone to try in your city (like theater shows, restaurants or activities). Giving advice to someone on a particular topic is always useful as well. There are many ways to keep the flow of information going and you will get better the more you focus on doing that.

How do I find my cornerstones of my power network?
Cornerstones are going to be hard to find initially but the more people you meet, the easier it will become. You'll figure out who is valuable, who is going to help you the most, and who is crucial to your success. Remember to set a goal before an event for the number of new people you'd like to meet. You can also set a goal for the number of people you want to meet in a one week period. If you

don't hit your goals, you must hold yourself accountable and continue trying.

How do I get my mentor to send me useful events?

Just let them know by saying, "I'm really interested in this (position, job, etc.) and I'm looking for networking events on these websites. Do you think those are good sites or would you try other ones?"

You can also ask them to connect you to somebody in a particular industry that can help you find events by asking, "Hey, do you happen to know anyone that goes to (industry) networking events?"

You could also discuss with them the idea of starting a weekly event e-mail group. Include some people you know and ask them to add others from their network.

Do you think it's better to go to networking events alone or with friends? What if I'm unmotivated to go alone?

I think that going with friends is fine as long as you don't use them as a 'life jacket.' If you're scared to approach strangers and start conversations, you will cling to your friend. This may make you feel more secure, but it will hardly help you gain new business contacts. I find that until you become more confident, it is better to go alone. If you are over twenty-one and drink alcohol, I would also suggest not drinking at networking events until you're confident. This ensures that you are not relying on a substance for false confidence (and will help you stay focused on your goals).

If you're unmotivated to go, think about all the opportunities that you might be missing. List out the companies and people that will be at the event and how it will positively affect your future. Also, if you find events that are focused on a field that you are passionate about, you will be more motivated.

Personal Challenge

Meet the Right People (5 days)

Step 1: Find two networking events to attend in the next five days. These events must have people in attendance that you NEED to meet. Use the sixteen websites from earlier in the chapter.

Step 2: Ask ten people to do an informational interview. You are focused. You are confident. You are ready to get that job. These steps will help you get it. Don't worry if people reject you or don't have time. Just keep asking. Once you get your first one you'll realize how easy it is.

Step 3: Write down the two events you are going to attend and how many informational interviews you plan to have in the next week. Be as specific as possible.

Tools & Tricks

Vsnap.com - This is an app and website I use to send people follow-up videos. It's more personal and will help people remember your face.

CardMunch - The most useful app I've ever had. It allows you to take a picture of a business card and save the contact info to your phone. It then automatically finds that person on LinkedIn and you can connect with them in one click.

Sadhguru (sadhguru.org) - The best public speaker I've ever witnessed and a master at mindfulness and meditation.

Chapter 9 - The Art of American Small Talk

"Fear is the mind killer." - *Frank Herbert*

"You don't learn to walk by following rules. You learn by doing, and falling over." - *Richard Branson*

The Two-Billion Dollar Man

Dr. Amarpreet Sawhney, or Amar, is the President and CEO of Ocular Therapeutix, Inc. This company focuses on unmet needs in ophthalmic surgical wound management and drug delivery. In short, he is the Richard Branson of medical entrepreneurship.

Previously, he was founder and CEO of biosurgery company Confluent Surgical (acquired by Covidien), then the Chairman of MarketRx (acquired by Cognizant), a provider of pharmaceutical marketing and sales analytics and intelligence, technology founder of Focal, Inc. (acquired by Genzyme) and Founder of Access Closure Inc. He is a member of the board of directors of Axtria, Ocular Therapeutix, Augmenix, and Incept LLC. Last but not least, Dr. Sawhney's innovations are the subject of over one hundred issued and pending patents.

Most important to note is that Amar's companies have added 1500 jobs and two billion dollars to the U.S. economy! The numbers are simply astounding, especially when accredited to just one man.

He also happens to be one of the nicest and wisest people I have ever had the pleasure of speaking with. His outlook on life worth emulating.

So how did his journey begin?

He came from a middle-class family in India, but was able to attend one of the best schools in the nation: The Indian Institute of

Technology. Admissions are very challenging, but a student and graduate of that school will come into contact plethora of business connections and career options. At the time of Amar's graduation, he had a few different good options in front of him. He had a job from campus placement, had gained admission to all the top management schools in India because of his scores on another competitive and very selective exam, and he got a fellowship from the University of Texas at Austin, which has one of the top ten chemical engineering programs.

Not one of his three options would have been a poor choice. Still, some were more secure than others. Amar chose the riskiest one: the fellowship at the University of Texas. It was the most unknown and intimidating choice. He didn't know many people in the States (certainly not in Texas) and cultural adjustment was going to be as difficult as the engineering studies—if not more so. However, he wanted to experience life in the United States, and knew if he didn't like it, he could always return to India.

So he arrived in Austin without a single acquaintance, nor even a place to live. Luckily, a student from the International Student Associations let him stay at his house for a couple days. With only five-hundred dollars in his pocket, no car and no knowledge of the city, Amar needed to figure out school registration and find a place to live. Understandably, it was quite a shock for him to just "parachute" in with so little support or knowledge of the situation.

Eventually, he found a couple new students like himself: unsure of the situation, and fairly confused. They decided to get an apartment together. Even though shops, groceries and even the school campus were a miserably long bus-ride away, they managed. Amar recognized that his struggles were not unique for an international student, and continued on with life.

When he completed his M.A. studies, he began to look for a job. He assumed that the job market was similar to that in India, where job availability is high, even for recent graduates. What a shock, then when Amar applied to thirty companies and twenty-nine dismissed him immediately because he didn't have a green card and they didn't know what to make of him. At the time, he was working on gynecological scar prevention, while everyone else was working on massive distillation columns and petrochemicals with companies like Chevron. He wasn't quite the laughing-stock of Texas, but no one really knew what to think of him, or his subject of expertise.

This is when he came to a fork in the road. Should he go back to India where he had plenty of opportunity, or continue to fight the uphill battle of acquiring employment in the States? Amar felt the pressure of working in a small, unknown field, and faced cultural barriers as a Sikh man in Texas.

Being the intelligent person he is, Amar asked his mentor and advisor, Jeff Hubble, to sit down and talk about this crucial decision. Surprisingly, Jeff told him he knew of an interesting project currently being done by a Ph.D. student. Jeff suggested that Amar work on it. Amar decided to take it, not knowing at the time that it would prove to be the defining point of his career. During the Ph.D. project, he and a partner developed an innovative new technology later licensed by a venture capital firm. Consequently, a job niche was created and Amar was the perfect candidate.

Amar's conscious decision to take the riskier and more demanding path resulted in his obtaining a job and visa. He believes that if he had simply been handed a visa just for getting a degree in America, he would be making tires in Midland, Michigan or working for DuPont. Facing adversity brought the best out in him and made him the person he is today.

The situation and circumstance surrounding Amar are not the only factors that shaped his experience. Amar is an eternal optimist, meaning he always tries to find a silver lining in moments of adversity. For example, he wears a turban every day of his life. You may think that, in a new country, blending in and avoiding physical displays of your own different culture would be wise. For Amar, it is not only a personal and cultural duty, but it distinguishes him from others: every single person he meets remembers him. Thus, his optimism and refusal to believe that something is wholly bad has helped him. Similarly, Amar is a very persistent person. Even if he cannot see the exact moment of success approaching on the horizon, he continues to pursue it. By combining optimism and persistence, he places himself well above the average member of the workforce.

This advice made a lasting impression on me and after speaking with him for just a short time, he had my eternal respect. I could easily see why he had been so successful in life, and I found myself wanting to help him in any way I could. I asked him how he had built this interpersonal skill and how he implements it into his day-to-day business networking. He replied that he is not conscious networker; he's *re*active, rather than active. He even said he got dragged into LinkedIn and Facebook but now has **thousands of contacts,** despite never uploading his email contact directory of about 7000 people. Still, he receives constant e-mails seeking career, entrepreneurial or even dating advice. Within this barrage of requests, Amar has noticed that few people take the time to actually help others. He makes sure that he is different. Amar believes that if you take a little bit of time to help others, there will be an eventual return of people popping out of the woodwork and saying, "Hey, that piece of advice really helped me. Thank you so much!"

This type of networking is both gratifying, and the most powerful. People have received guidance or help and they are now willing to help in return. He also makes sure to tell people that he's not *expecting* anything in return, because this a short-sighted way of looking at the relationship. He just does it because when a favor is passed along, the world becomes a better place.

Quite simply, Amar has a remarkable view on life, which has been helpful to people across the globe. I believe this a key driver to his success. Look at society in general: if you only have 'takers,' the percentage of people taking information, goods, etc. from others is too high. Conversely, if you have people who give back more than what they take, an excess of goods accumulates. Both are necesary: the machinery, and the oil that keeps it lubricated. Otherwise, we all live separate lives, taking without returning. Yes, the world can go on that way but it's not a fun place to be.

Instead, I suggest you try to give back as much as possible like Amar.

Start Learning The Art

Small talk is the must-have skill when networking or socializing. Learning the art will build your confidence, help you bond with strangers and most of all, make them remember you. By the end of this chapter, you will be able to approach any social or networking setting with confidence.

First, you must say goodbye to shyness. You need to be open to talking to anyone! You will feel uncomfortable and a little weird, but that is part of the process of changing your normal behavior and stretching out of your comfort zone. This skill will allow you to meet more people, find more opportunities and become more successful.

At this point, you know where to find events and how to give yourself goals for those events. The only thing left is to understand how to turn your small talk conversations into job offers.

So why do people small talk?

Very simply, it builds a bridge. By exchanging basic information through light and casual conversation, you can connect with anyone, from anywhere. In a short amount of time, you can learn the basics about someone. From there, you can quickly get to know someone on a personal level by finding out what they enjoy doing or mutual interests. I've done this with people from all over the world and constantly attend international events because I love identifying these 'bridges.' Sometimes the most random, obscure connections can produce amazing links to people from around the world. You need to understand, though, that small talk is different in every country. Each culture has its own manner of engaging in small talk, and most importantly, its own topics which are considered appropriate and inappropriate.

Why else is small talk important in a business environment?

First and foremost, it displays your communication skills, which are important to any employer. Employers look for people who can converse effectively with others because employees often work on teams. It also demonstrates your level of confidence to others. If you can start a conversation with anyone and make a lasting impression, that is impressive. This skill will open up new business opportunities, new friends and even assist you in the dating game. You'll see that this skill is one of the most important to your personal and career development. Just by learning how to small talk effectively, will easily double your job opportunities.

Building Personal Connections

Remember, out of all of those reasons to engage in small talk, the most fundamental is to build personal connections quickly. Always be focused on others and how you can help them. By quickly asking other people about their interests and encouraging them to talk, you facilitate that relationship. Everyone loves to talk about themselves and usually won't run out of things to say. From there, it's your job to find a similar interest.

Once that mutual interest is found, I strongly believe that people can build a personal connection in five minutes or less. Then the conversation becomes a simple flow of information: you ask a question, he or she responds and perhaps ask you the same question. Whether you're discussing 'company culture,' what they do for fun, or the wildest experienced they ever had, your conversation will have plenty of momentum so long as each party is motivated to speak about a topic they find interesting.

In my case, if someone starts talking about poetry, I would be relatively bored as I have little interest in the subject. However, I will continue to ask questions about the arts and try to find a mutual interest, like painting. If they enjoyed painting, I could tell them about this cool spot in another part of the city where you can drink wine and paint with a fun group of people. Then I immediate follow up by pulling out my phone, getting their email and sending them the name of the place. Almost instantly I've built a personal connection with this other person.

Amazing, right?

With practice you will be able to do this with anyone, even the most important CEO.

What do you talk about?

When you start a conversation with someone you've never met, it's important to begin with light topics—topics that couldn't possibly start an argument or cause controversy. Your goal of every conversation should be to find a similar interest, something that can use to build a connection with this stranger (not antagonize him). Too often, I observe people walk directly up to another person and say, "Hi, what do you do for work?" It is best not to start a conversation this way. You can discuss professions, perhaps not right at the start. People hear that question all the time, and it isn't that memorable. Try to discuss something more fun and personal.

Any of these topics are appropriate small talk topics to discuss with Americans:

- Travel
- Movies
- Music
- Theatre
- Books
- Food
- Entertainment

- Sports
- Travel

You might think that these topics are more useful for social settings when you're trying to make friends, but it's not true. Talking about these topics at professional events is normal and a great way to form a business connection.

There are many other topics but those are some ideas to start you off with. I especially suggest that you try discussing your travel stories. Most people enjoy traveling, be it to their cabin in the summer, or to exotic foreign cities. In that vein, your stories from abroad will be new and interesting to most and provide them with useful information. As you recall, networking works when there is a constant flow of useful information.

Topics To Avoid

Every country has different *faux pas* topics that you need to avoid. Bringing these topics up can absolutely ruin business and personal opportunities.

Any of these topics are inappropriate small talk topics to discuss with Americans:

- Money
- Sex
- Politics
- Religion
- Family Problems (i.e. divorce)
- Death
- Economic Problems
- Terrorism & War

For example, in India it is common to ask "How's the health of your family?" This question would not be well-received in the States, as that kind of 'intimate' question would be deemed inappropriate.

Money is a touchy topic and you need to treat it delicately. In some countries it is very common to ask, "How much do you make?" However, if you ask an America that question it is considered rude and offensive. Like family matters, we tend to keep things closer to the vest.

Sex is another topic highlights the American feeling on impropriety. What may be easily, casually discussed in a European country, for example, would cause an Americana to blush. You might be noticing the general theme of the American idea of 'personal' information. We tend not to share this information in a first meeting, so like sex, family problems, divorce and death are not mentioned. It may be confusing to see 'politics' on the list as well, because you likely hear people talking about politics quite often. However, I exclude it from the list of small talk topics because it can very easily lead to an argument. Discussion of economic matters and opinions could lead to a similar outcome. Imagine, for example, that you happen to love the President and his policies, and someone cannot stand him. Sparks will fly. The same applies to religion: with such a variety and intensity of opinions regarding religion, it is best to just leave the subject along in an initial small talk session.

If someone else brings up one of these topics, then it is your job to steer the conversation away in another direction. The last thing you want is a feeling of negativity, and it is better to make the conversation slightly awkward for a moment than to fall into a tense discussion of an uncomfortable topic. Remember, the goal of your conversation is to build that connection where eventually can lead to a job, not a shouting match.

Small Talk Cheat Sheet

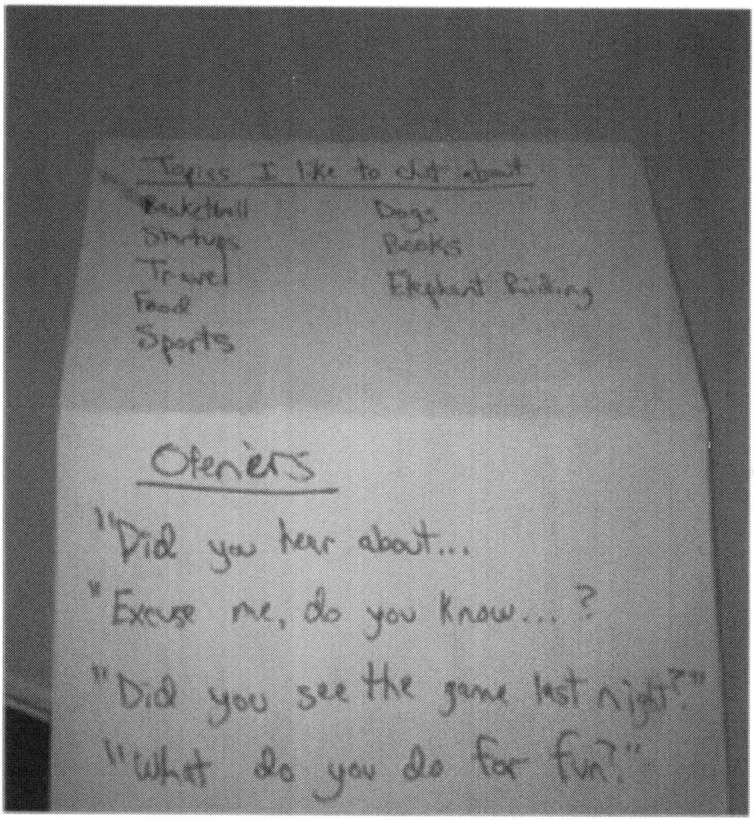

Why do students love it when a professor allows them to use a "cheat sheet" for an exam?

It allows them to have on-hand notes and information that are tough to recall on the spot. These notes could even determine if the student passes or fails the exam, either by providing the information, or by building the student's confidence such that he or she does not begin to falter when nervous.

So why should life be any different?

We all get worried in new social situations, and in our nervousness sometimes forget what's really important. We forget what to say, how to say it and what our goals are. Fortunately, there is a solution that will help you (as it helped me) become more confident and out-going: the small talk cheat sheet.

When I got nervous, all I had to do was pull my little sheet out and quickly find something to start a conversation. It was a great reminder.

So how do you make a small talk cheat sheet?

It's very simple. Get a piece of paper and fold it in quarters. You will have eight sections (one for each topic). In each part, write different key things to remember. I make these sheets for different social situations and each has it's own unique tips, tricks and reminders. You can write whatever you want but this is how I usually break it down:

- 10 things you enjoy talking about
- 10 things you'd like to learn about others
- 5 openers or things that you could say to start a conversation
- 5 current events or 'hot' topics
- 5 personal stories
- 5 ways to help others
- reasons to overcome your fears
- goals for event

I believe that the hardest part of a conversation is having the courage to start it. It is intimidating to have to open with an engaging, interesting topic. Of course, that's usually the first thing that people forget when they are nervous. So if you tend to have trouble doing that, I'd suggest trying each of these conversation openers:

- "Hi, I'm new to (city name) and am looking for amazing new experience this weekend. Do you have any suggestions?" (works even if you have lived there for 10 years)
- "Did you do/like/dislike the reading we had to do?" (for students)
- "Did you hear about...?" (refer to a recent event most will have knowledge about)

- "Do you know____________?" (make a connection with a mutual acquaintance)
- "Do you always get the same drink?" (coffee shop introduction)
- "I like your shirt/hat/sweater/shoes, etc. Where did you get them?" (everyone loves compliments)

Find out which works best for you and reuse it. Remember 20% of the things you say to start a conversation with will lead to 80% of your success.

Entering The Conversation

Sometimes entering a conversation can feel like jumping off a cliff. I'm here to tell you that you have to be ready to take the plunge! You have to be sure, though, just as with cliff diving, to keep a specific form so you don't end up falling flat on your face.

The way you enter a conversation will give others an initial impression to you and can decide your success or failure. So how do you begin?

Start by looking for people who are already talking. Most people are shocked when they learned this. It sounds crazy: you don't wanna interrupt anyone, right?

Wrong.

People already engaged in conversation are more open to talking to someone new. If you try to approach someone that isn't talking, you might not have success: they might be having a bad day, might not want to talk to anyone, or they might be terrified to talk to a stranger. If that's the case, nothing you do will change that. If instead you find people that are already talking, they will probably accept you and allow you to join the discussion.

When you enter the group you want to **establish eye contact** with someone and smile. The 'smiling American' joke has some truth to it: Americans smile all the time! Failing to do so in an introductory setting like this will make you appear cold and unfriendly. A warm smile, on the other hand, shows your confidence and that you will be a valuable addition to the group. You also want to be the first to introduce yourself. Don't be caught standing awkwardly on the edge of the circle, waiting for someone to ask you what your name is. This shows a complete lack of confidence.

Let me reiterate: you need to make an assertive entrance into the group, establish eye contact with someone, say 'hello' and then ask an open ended question. This can be any questions that requires more than a one-word answer (for example, asking "Did you have a nice weekend?" will get a shorter response than "What did you do this weekend?"). Any of the "opener" examples will work and easily start a conversation.

You also want to focus on remembering other people's names. This can be really hard to do if you're worrying about entering the conversation and thinking about what you're going to say. As you build your confidence and eliminate your doubts, it will become easier to remember other people's names. The majority of people can't do this, so if you build that skill, you will continue to differentiate yourself. Remember a person's name show to a new contact that you care about them, which is important to building a relationship quickly.

5 Tips to Remembering Names

1. At the moment of introduction, focus on the person's face and get a clear picture of them in your head. Associate the name to their face because it will help you remember them in the long run.
2. Immediately repeat their name. After you hear it, respond with, "Nice to meet you (name)."

3. Say their name periodically throughout the conversation. Doing this will help you memorize it. You'll notice every sales person uses this trick.
4. Think of someone you know with the same name, or something that rhymes with the name (useful for unfamiliar/foreign names).
5. Always use a person's name when closing a conversation.

Four Talking Techniques To Master

1. Personal Elevator Pitch

The goal of this pitch is to give other people an accurate overview of yourself in thirty to sixty seconds. It should explain your background and expertise in a quick and memorable fashion. At some point during a conversation, someone will probably ask you why you are at the event, what you do, or what your background is. A this instance, you will pull out your elevator pitch. For instance, my pitch would be something like:

"I'm an author and the founder of Culture Adapt. I help international individuals achieve their dreams and succeed in American business. I ended up in this career because I'm really passionate about different cultures, business and helping others. I grew up in Northern Vermont, have lived in Hong Kong, China, have employed people from eight different countries, and have travelled to more than thirty countries."

Boom! That would take me less than thirty seconds to say, and anyone listening would know a lot about me. I give a couple of interesting facts, discuss how I got into my field and even say where I'm from. I took some time to create this pitch, wrote it down and practiced it over and over again until it felt natural. You need to do the same thing.

Think about what makes you an expert, particularly memorable or unique. Next, write your own pitch; it should be roughly one or two paragraphs in length. Remember to add some emotion to it, too. If you speak in a bland and monotone fashion, people are not going to remember you. Finally, practice it in front of the mirror until you have it memorized and it feels right. You can record yourself and ask for feedback from mentors or peers to perfect this pitch. Now you are ready to use it at a networking event.

2. Active Listening

This technique will help you build a relationship with others. Active listening includes eye contact, head nodding, hand gestures, and asking follow-up questions. Asking follow-up questions to what others have shared will facilitate the conversation. If you don't ask these questions the conversation, can trail off and you will be left awkwardly looking at your shoes until the person leaves to talk to someone else. Let's avoid that scenario! Instead, you will listen for facts, feelings and key words to build on. For instance, if someone says, "After I stopped working for those jerks," it *probably* means that he disliked his former employer or the job in general. Even if he wasn't so specific as to call them 'jerks,' you will notice that he used the past tense. This tells you that, regardless of the reason why, he no longer works at that company. If you pick up on these little hints throughout a conversation, your new contact will understand that you're listening closely and responding to the information. This, of course, encourages them to share more.

3. Personal Storytelling

Everyone single person has unique and interesting stories to tell. It's up to you to improve your own storytelling skills. These stories can be about your background, interests, or experiences. Personally, I love telling stories and encourage you to embrace it because it provides such great, small window into your life. For instance, when someone brings up travel, I love telling them about the time I went to Chiang Mai, Thailand to ride elephants, play with tigers and handle cobras. It's exciting, interesting and helps get conversations flowing.

I want you to think about your own unique personal stories and write ten of them down on paper. By writing them down, it will help you form them, describe the most interesting parts and remember them more easily for later use. You can even add your favorites to your small talk cheat sheet.

4. Directing Conversation Towards Job Opportunities

Once you have built a connection with someone, and that person wants to help you, you can start directing the conversation towards job opportunities. When that time comes, you should start by casually bringing up professional topics. The key work here is *casually:* you never want to directly say, "Does your company have any job openings?" or "Do you have any problems at work that I can help fix?"

As I mentioned earlier, being that direct will turn most people off. Instead, you want to ask a question like, "What are the most interesting problems you're facing in your position?"

Questions like this inspire people to think about their own issues, instead of yours, and it doesn't feel so intrusive or direct. Then once they delve into the topic, you can more easily figure out how to help them. You can also ask a person how they got their position or how they became successful. Most people have successes they are proud of and love talking about them.

Indirect questions like these will help you direct the conversation without making someone feel like it's all about you. With practice you will learn how to steer these talks towards something that can be beneficial to your job search.

Exiting The Conversation

So you know what topics to start with, topics to avoid, how to steer the conversation, and how to build your confidence. Now you must learn to know when and how to exit a conversation. Remember that you have a specific goal for every event and that you need to manage your time to reach that goal. If you are at an hour-long event and your goal is to meet twelve important people, you need to make sure you're not talking to anyone for more than five minutes. With this kind of mindset, you will always maximize your time in conversations.

If you become proficient at small talk, you'll be able to quickly understand what a person does and how they might be able to help you. You will learn how to quickly assess the value of the person or people you are speaking with. If they have little or no relevance to your goal, it is time to exit.

Sadly, many people get stuck talking to one or two people for entire events and miss the opportunity to speak with the VP standing next to them. Realize that ending a conversation is not rude; it is practical. You can always speak to someone again if you've built the relationship on a mutual interest or have helped them. Still, when it is time to exit a conversation, it's important to do it politely or you could completely ruin the relationship. Make sure that you get their contact information so can follow-up with them. If you don't, you're missing out on great opportunities and your network will never grow.

These are the steps to follow:

1. Restate something you found interesting about the person or conversation
2. Invite them to speak again
3. Exchange contact information (if you don't have business cards, get some made)
4. Establish eye contact again and smile
5. Say, "Nice meeting you (name)", shake their hand and walk away

It seems simple, but many people don't do this properly and it costs them opportunities.

You now know all the skills and techniques necessary to master the art of American small talk. Follow the advice and you will feel comfortable after just a few conversations.

Questions and Actions

How long did it take you to get over your fear and approach other people?
All throughout high school and college I was scared to approach people I didn't know. I was comfortable with the people I knew, and didn't see the value of building my small talk skills at that time. For years, I did not have the confidence to approach strangers. Luckily, my move to Georgia forced me to develop them. When I was put in that situation where small talk was necessary for me to 'survive,' I stopped caring about my fears and just kept trying. Over about three months my confidence skyrocketed, at which point I was able to approach and start a conversation with absolutely anyone.

How do you enter a group of people that are already talking without being rude?
You can do this a number of ways. If you just burst into the group and loudly say something, that can be pretty rude. On the other hand, there really there is no perfect time to enter. If you try to find the 'perfect opening' you are going to end up awkwardly standing at the edge of the group. I've seen people that are super energetic, enter a conversation by putting their arms around two people and saying, "Hey! What you guys are talking about?" I've seen others smile, nod and simply say 'hello.' Both work really well.

I cannot imagine starting a conversation by suddenly joining a circle and saying, "Hey, did you hear about..." Does that really work?
Yes, it absolutely works. Using current events in this line works really well. For instance, I remember using the RedBull Space Dive as an

opener. I would walk up to a group of people and excitedly say, "Hey guys, did you hear about the RedBull Space Dive? How crazy was that?"

Instantly, that conversation would shift to my topic. It didn't matter what they were talking about before I entered the conversation. My topic was so new and interesting that everyone wanted to discuss it.

Don't listen to the 'what if' thoughts. Just try it like I did in Georgia, and see for yourself.

How do I know if I've offended someone and if I do, how can I recover?

If an American abruptly ends a conversation, you may have offended them. Usually the person will look shocked and say something to you. Americans are fairly open about their feelings and when they've been offended. However, you can counter this by apologizing and explaining your actual meaning. Sometimes cultural differences can cause awkward moments but if you remain calm and in good humor, I have no doubt that you can recover. Heck, I'd even suggest trying a little rejection therapy with this. If you purposely offended someone (in a minor way), could you keep your cool and maintain the relationship? I bet so.

Personal Challenge

Talk to Three Strangers (1 day)

You're an amazing person with an interesting background and awesome personal stories. If you're not talking to new people, you're doing them a disservice by not allowing them to get to know you.

I'm challenging everyone that reads this to speak to **three strangers in the next 24 hours!**

This could be someone at the coffee shop, a grocery store, in a class, a bookstore...or even that person you have a crush on. It doesn't matter. Just take action in the next 24 hours and you'll see how easy it is!

Chapter 10: Overcoming Culture Shock Faster

"The growth markets of the world are clearly overseas." - *John F. Smith, Jr. Chairman of General Motors*

"Yes, we live in an interconnected world, but there is someone making the connections. It could be you." - *Frans Johansson, Author of The Medici Effect and The Click Moment*

Bridging The Gap

I had just arrived to New York City for a mysterious event being held by the innovation consulting company, The Medici Group. I had been invited by chance after meeting the founder. At a Harvard event, I had told best-selling author Frans Johansson that I wanted to cure culture shock. Later, we had spoken on the phone and he decided to invite me. However, he provided *zero* details about what was going to happen at this event. I was going in blind.

When I arrived at the office, I rode the elevator to the 14th floor with a couple others. One was an archeologist who had recently discovered the oldest piece of art in Europe, and the other was a hedge fund manager. I could tell already that the event was going to be awesome.

We arrived upstairs and were each given a neon colored sash with a name-tag, then asked to mingle for a little bit. I tried to meet as many of the guests as I could, and found that they were leaders in different fields: engineering, business, entrepreneurship, acting, art, film, finance, etc. After about fifteen minutes of mingling (during which time I connected with about fifteen people), they called us all together to start the event.

We did an icebreaker exercise in which the entire group was asked to connect with one another in a unique way. For example, a successful artist who had chosen to live on the street with his dog (I promise I am not making this up) connected with a financial manager through their mutual love of dogs.

Imagine that: two people, with two completely different backgrounds and outlooks on life were able to make a simple, binding connection. The point of this exercise was to get everyone thinking outside the box, and to make connections that you might normally overlook. After the warm-up, we were broken into teams (based on sash color). Then we actually formulated innovative consulting for a real company that had invited as well. The process was like nothing I'd ever heard of or participated in, and I loved it.

By the end of the day I had learned that The Medici Group is based on the principle that diversity drives innovation (a belief to which I personally ascribe). The events of the day had strengthened this belief as I watched teams of people with different ethnic, language, educational and professional backgrounds make connections and create amazingly innovative ideas. In all, this one day in New York reinforced just how valuable culture adaptation is to this generation of professionals.

So now it's your turn. Want to grow as a person? Make new friends? Accelerate your career? Drive global innovation? Start learning how to bridge cultural gaps and adapt to new situations quickly.

Prince Akeem

If you've never watched the 1988 classic comedy, "Coming to America" (starring Eddie Murphy), you should.

The movie is about Prince Akeem and his assistant, Semmi, who leave their home country on a quest to America to find Prince Akeem a wife. Upon arrival they decide to live in a 'real' American neighborhood (Queens, New York) and get 'real' American jobs at a fast food restaurant. However, the two men approach the adventure in very different ways. On one hand, Prince Akeem enters the country with an open mind, is grateful for any experience he can find and learns as much as he can from Americans. He is always happy, and ultimately becomes successful (and even finds a wife)!

On the other hand, Semmi constantly complains about America's differences from his homeland, refuses to experience anything new or even interact with Americans. He feels homesick, alone, out-of-place and finally returns to his home country without seeing any success. This entertaining movie paints a perfect picture of two outcomes that can happen when a foreign national moves to a new country. What Semmi was succumbing to is known as 'culture shock,' but luckily, his experience does not have to foreshadow your own.

The Four Phases of Culture Shock

Culture shock by definition is "the personal disorientation a person may feel when experiencing an unfamiliar way of life due to immigration or a visit to a new country, or to a move between social environments also a simple travel to another type of life."[1] It can make you feel depressed, lonely, frustrated, less confident, left out and homesick.

This feeling affects not only your personal life, but also your business life as well. You will be less productive, feel out-of-place and not as intelligent as you actually are. You may lose out on promotions, raises and other opportunities that you would have noticed in a different state of mind. For these reasons, it is crucial that you understand stages of culture shock, how you personally fit into them, and how you can overcome them. I can't stress the importance of this enough because if you do nothing, you will waste valuable months or years of your career.

Stage 1 - The Honeymoon

Culture shock affects all foreign nationals to some degree and typically starts after your first three or four weeks in America. This first three-to-four week phase is known as 'the Honeymoon.' A honeymoon is the short vacation taken immediately after a couple gets married, and American's joke that it is the best part of a marriage and everything gets worse after that. Think of your first three-to-four weeks in America as a honeymoon. You love everything! It's new, big, beautiful and exciting. Fast food is available on every corner, and you are surrounded by shops, sites and things to do. But then something happens. You start noticing little differences between American culture and your own. When you start to feel annoyed by these little idiosyncrasies, the honeymoon phase is over.

Stage 2 - Confusion

All the little things have added up and you are now feeling depressed. The elements of American culture that were initially interesting and different are now just frustrating—even infuriating. Daily details like the language barrier, stark differences in public hygiene, traffic safety, food accessibility and quality may heighten the sense of disconnection from the surroundings. You find yourself wound up in negative thoughts like:

"What the heck is a quarter? Why don't they write 'twenty-five' on it, if that's what they mean?"

"84 degrees *Fahrenheit*? What a ridiculous number! Why is America the only country using that system?"

"Miles? Feet? Inches? Why do they have to be so difficult?"

"What is this 'Family Guy' show? The humor doesn't make any sense, and I can barely understand the characters' accents! Why is it funny?"

"Why do they joke about each others mom's? It's rude and doesn't make sense."

You feel awkward, out of place and miss your home country and culture. The only thing in the world you want is to go back home.

On top of all this, you find yourself starting to dislike all Americans in general. How are you suppose to succeed in school or work if you dislike the people and culture around you?

Stage 3 - Adjustment

After some time (usually six to twelve months), you will grow accustomed to America and develop routines. You'll know what to expect in most situations and the host country no longer feels all that new. You'll start to develop problem-solving skills for dealing with American culture and begin to accept the American's ways with a positive attitude. American culture begins to make sense, and negative reactions and responses to the culture are reduced. [3]

Stage 4 - Mastery

The next phase can only be accomplished once you feel completely comfortable in America. Mastery does not mean total conversion; people keep many traits from their home culture, such as accents and language use, holiday celebration and humor style. Still, they begin to adopt certain elements of American culture, or are able to switch back-and-forth between the two cultural identities as needed. This is often referred to as the biculturalism stage. The most successful immigrants in America have persevered and reached the 'Mastery' phase only through years of hard work.

Culture shock will inevitably happen to you, and every other foreign national entering the U.S. this year. It will affect any person who is brave enough to leave his or her home culture and begin life in an unfamiliar country. This does not have to hinder your success, nor should it be used as an excuse for failure. Instead, it is up to you to minimize the time it takes you to progress from your 'honeymoon' to the 'adjustment' phase.

Are You Culturally Fluent?

I define cultural fluency as one's ability to easily understand and connect with people of another culture, while being aware of the ways the culture operates in communication and conflict. This awareness must then lead to the ability to respond effectively to those differences. And just like any other skill, you need to educate yourself and work hard to improve.

It's important to understand that English-language fluency does *not* equal cultural fluency, nor does it mean that you are guaranteed success in America. Yes, communication depends on the ease with which you use the language, but you cannot rely on it exclusively. Each culture consists of millions of minute behaviors and interactions, characteristics and cognitive constructs of a particular social, ethnic or age group. These things are typically learned through a lifelong process of socialization. Without them, someone can appear very foreign even when speaking fluently. Because you don't have the luxury or being raised within your new culture, you have to quickly pick up the basics of this 'lifelong process of socialization.' Quickly identifying patterns in American culture will help you determine which behaviors and characteristics will help you fit in and become successful. Though it will require you to completely change many of your behaviors and will feel strange at first, I believe that it can (and must) be done.

Let me now share with you my secret method for shortening your path to cultural fluency.

EVOLVE - Six Steps to Cultural Fluency

"I've lived in the U.S. for a while now, and I still feel isolated! I am unsure how to meet new people...and even more unsure how to communicate with Americans in social settings. I think the easiest solution is to just find friends from my home country."

I've heard this line too many times. Whether it is said by an Indian guy in Boston, a Japanese couple in Virginia or an American woman in China, the feelings and experience are the same. To leave your home country, language and culture behind is challenging enough, and then you must adapt to a new, unfamiliar culture. It can be overwhelming. That does not mean, however, that your experience has to be an unpleasant one. You can do more than just **survive** in a new country; you can thrive and succeed!

My travels to thirty-some countries, and experience as an expat and international student have helped me identify what it takes to bridge cultural gaps quickly. Though you will encounter all kinds of cultural oddities, embarrassments and misunderstandings in your time abroad, it is my belief that, with these six steps, you will quickly EVOLVE and become culturally fluent in any culture you choose.

1. Embrace Fear

I've discussed this throughout the book, and will continue to stress the importance of overcoming your fears. In a new culture, each day can lead to an nerve-wracking situations. It's not your job to avoid those situations; your responsibility is to *react* to them differently.

Try these three steps, to start:

- Write down ten situations that are intimidating or frightening to you
- Pick one of these situations
- Before you can talk yourself out of it, just follow through. Carry out the action
- Check it off the list
- Move on to the next item

For example, you could go back to the coffee shop and speak to the barista, strike up a conversation with a random good-looking person at bookstore, try that food that looks terrible, or even give a public speech in front of fifty people. Keep a record of what fears you have and constantly try to overcome them. I like to do one thing a day that scares me.

2. Venture Towards the Unknown

Once you've begun to accept that new situations will be intimidating, it is time to challenge yourself! The second step involves extending beyond the routine you've established.
Can you think of such a situation in your own life abroad? When so far from home, we often cling to routine as a means of feeling more secure and familiar in our surroundings. Yet in doing so we are often missing out.

Try one of these:

- Taking an alternative route to work/school. You may see a new restaurant, store, park, etc. that catches your eye
- Join a sports team or exercise group: you'll be meeting new people, and getting fit!
- Go to an American sporting event or concert. Who knows, you might like it.

3. Overcome preconceived notions

It is very easy to make assumptions about other people; easier still when everyone seems very different from you. Building prejudice barriers will do nothing to help you connect to others, though. Be open to meeting anyone.

Try this thought exercise when walking around town, sitting on the bus, etc.

If you see someone who looks particularly different (i.e. skin color, hair style, tattoos/piercings, etc.), create a story for that person.

- What is his/her name?
- How old is he/she?
- What does he/she do for a living?
- What does he/she do for fun?
- What kind of pet does he/she have?
- What is that pet's name?
- What is his/her favorite film or TV show?

When you create this backstory, that stranger begins to look more familiar.

1 Learn about your new Home

When I lived in China, everything I learned about the culture was self-taught. This is what most people do and it takes time. It is an important process, though, as learning the basic principles of a culture will help you achieve fluency faster. The basics can be understood by educating yourself on Hofstede's theory of cultural dimensions.

Professor Geert Hofstede developed his original theory through factor analysis, examining results of a worldwide survey of employee values by IBM in the 1960s and 1970s. The theory was one of the first that could be quantified, and could be used to explain observed differences between cultures. In brief, it proposes six dimensions along which cultural values could be analyzed: individualism-collectivism; uncertainty avoidance; power distance (strength of social hierarchy); masculinity-femininity (task orientation versus person-orientation); long-term orientation (to cover aspects of values not discussed in the original paradigm), and indulgence versus self-restraint.

Further research has refined some of the original dimensions, and introduced the difference between country-level and individual-level data in analysis. [4]

As you read through the cultural dimensions that define America, think about how they might differ from your own.

Power distance - the extent to which the less powerful members of institutions and organizations within a country expect and accept that power is distributed unequally.

The American creed is "liberty and justice for all." This is why there is a focus on equal rights in all aspects of American society and government. Within American organizations, hierarchy is established for convenience, superiors are easily accessible and managers rely on their employees for their expertise. Communication is informal, direct and participative. This explains why America's score is relatively low on this dimension (40).

Individualism - the degree of interdependence a society maintains among its members.

I've mentioned this throughout the book, but America is a highly individualistic culture. This relates to their score of 91 on this dimension. People are only expected to look after themselves and their immediate family members. Americans are accustomed to doing business with, or interacting, with complete strangers. This is why most Americans are not shy to approach others or ask for information. In the business world, employees are expected to be self-reliant and motivated. Hiring and promotion decisions are mostly based on merit or evidence of what one has done or can do.

Masculinity / Femininity - what motivates people, wanting to be the best (masculine) or liking what you do (feminine).

This dimension has nothing to do with gender, but rather competitiveness. The United States scores a 62, which designates it as a "masculine" society. Americans talk freely about their successes and achievements and strive to "be the best they can be." Many Americans "live to work" so they can earn more money and gain a higher status. This is not the mindset you should have.

Uncertainty avoidance - The extent to which the members of a culture feel threatened by ambiguous or unknown situations and have created beliefs and institutions that try to avoid these.
Americans tend to be more tolerant of ideas and opinions and promote free speech. There is also an innovative mindset that encourages Americans to try new and different things, whether it pertains to technology, business practices, or food. Therefore America, scores a 46 on this dimension.

Long-term orientation - the extent to which a society shows a pragmatic future-oriented perspective rather than a conventional short-term point of view.
The United States scores a 29 on this dimension, and is therefore a short-term oriented culture. Most businesses focus on short-term goals, usually reviewed on quarterly basis. This results in Americans striving to make quick results in the workplace. Americans also tend to think short-term in their personal lives. [5]

I suggest you research the dimensions more and use the Hofstede website in the "Tools & Resources" section of this chapter to investigate your own country.

Of course, there is always immense value in learning about a culture from within. This can be a wonderful conversation starter: most people like talking about the aspects of their own country and society.

- Ask an American to describe the culture to you in one of two sentences, or in 'bumper sticker' form (short and concise, like the phrases seen on car bumper stickers). It may be difficult for them to narrow it down, but once they do, the response might be eye opening to you. I would suggest trying to do the same for your own home country, too!

5. Value Patience & Tolerance

If you are a foreign national and new to the United States, you have likely noticed the striking diversity of the population. Though we still have some tension around race relations and religious and sexual preferences, Americans by and large show a heightened sense of political correctness. This has a lot of implications for our society as a whole, but most noticeable are its effects on communication. This means that some topics or styles of humor are not acceptable. In this case, your awareness will be key in understanding the culture, and avoiding giving offense.

- Be careful of labels like Black (rather than African-American), fireman (firefighter, for both men and women), Indian (Native American), Chicano (Latino, or specific nationality): some people don't mind these designations, while others may be greatly offended.

- As I said in my discussion of small talk, politics and religion are touchy topics in the United States. Among friends and peers, it isn't usually a problem, but when networking or meeting new people, watch what you say. Every one of these points, of course, is situational. Ultimately, you are the best judge of what will be acceptable, or unbelievable.

6. Enjoy Your New World

This last step may seem like the easiest: just *enjoy!* And yet, this relaxed, confident enjoyment is likely just what you're struggling with. So take a step back: the uncomfortable moments we discussed in steps one and two: do they define you?

No.

They are small pieces of your life—of that one day—that add up. Keep this in mind while you are pushing yourself to be more adventurous and outgoing. Some days will not feel successful, but don't dwell on those days. Focus instead on the things that no person can take from you: your courage, your intelligence, your experience, the love of your family and friends. These things will always stay with you and are what make you truly successful. Remember that, keep life in perspective and you will feel even more ready to try something new.

Questions & Actions

I feel like Americans are not culturally sensitive and it's hard to become friends with them. Why?

Some Americans will be more open-minded than others, just like any other country in the world. Most people don't educate themselves on cultural differences and therefore don't understand them. If you meet someone like this, try to help them. Tell them about the EVOLVE methodology and Hofstede's cultural dimensions. You will be making the world a better place.

Why is it important to be able to adapt to different cultures?

If you build this skill, you will be able to work anywhere in the world. You will be extremely valuable to global companies and they will seek you out. You'll notice that you become happier in foreign countries and be able to build relationships with anyone. It will improve you both personally and professionally. I want you to give yourself a goal to become friends with people from at least 20 different countries. Once you do that, you'll be well on your way to becoming a global citizen.

Personal Challenge
Cook An American Meal (1 Day)

This challenge can be really fun. I want you to embrace American culture by cooking a traditional American meal.

What is that?

Well, we like take foods from all around the world and pretend that they are our own. (Lasagna, burritos, etc.) Go for a dish that is particularly foreign to you. Perhaps the ingredients aren't used in your home country, or maybe it has been recommended by a friend or classmate. When I was in China, I never shopped at Western grocery stores to ensure that I would try as many new foods as possible. I experimented with all kinds of dishes with traditional Chinese ingredients, spices and sauces.

Chicken feet? Made it. Stinky tofu? Made it. Cow intestine? Made it.

I also made more 'normal' stir fry and noodle dishes, too, but I'm using those examples to get my point across. If you're having trouble thinking of a truly American meal, **these are some ideas for you:** barbecued ribs, buffalo wings, grits (southern food), western omelet, clam chowder, meatloaf and mashed potatoes, chicken pot pie, pancakes with maple syrup (only use the syrup from Vermont), or Philly cheesesteaks.

Feel free to do this challenge with someone else or invite others over for dinner. Then you can all share your culinary experience! Go beyond your comfort zone and see where it takes you.

Tools & Resources

The Hofstede Center (geert-hofstede.com/countries.html) - The Hofstede Center's website provides a tool to compare your country's cultural dimensions with any other country.

Chapter 11 - Grow Your Online Network

"Where recommendations have replaced references, connections trump cover letters and the résumé is a soon-to-be relic–who and what you know are critical." -*Coca Cola Company*

"Instead of telling the world what you're eating for breakfast, you can use social networking to do something that's meaningful." - *Edward Norton*

Social Media - A Waste of Time?

"Why the heck should I improve my LinkedIn profile?" I asked my friend John.

At the time, my LinkedIn profile looked like a desolate wasteland, completely empty save for my current title and education history. My lackluster profile was a result of my complete dislike of social media. I didn't have a Twitter account, never used YouTube and barely ever used Facebook. I saw it as a waste of my time; I valued efficiency and was under the impression that everyone used these sites because they had nothing better to do.

"Well, what if you ever want to start your own business or change jobs? You're going to need to use LinkedIn a lot. Why not set it up now? " He replied. I brushed off his comment.

"Eh, whatever. I'll be able to do it without that stuff. I read business books all the time and they never mention it." Despite wanting to start a company, I actually believed that social media would be of no real use to me. Why waste five minutes connecting with people on LinkedIn or tweeting when I could be writing a business plan?

For two years, I continued to believe that I had more valuable things to do with my time than tweet or "socialize" on LinkedIn. But then I really took a giant leap and started a company, with almost zero business knowledge. I slowly learned how to build a website, sell, retain customers, and make money. Sure enough, a giant part of making money was based on marketing—a skill I had never been taught. Soon enough, I discovered that some types of marketing were really expensive. For example, a group deal with RueLaLa allowed them to take about thirty percent of whatever we made. At the same time, we were using Google ads that were costly and didn't produce enough results, just like the adds in a local newspaper (a complete waste of money).

Trying to get sales leads was a difficult process, too. We had to do online research, cold-call companies or attend networking events. Everything was either costing money or taking up time. Frustrated with the situation, I began to brainstorm other options. That was when I realized that social media was the only free kind of marketing and one of the best ways to reach new customers or sales leads. I thought back to what John had told me years earlier and realized the HUGE mistake I had made. A person's social presence grows exponentially and by doing nothing for that two year period, I had probably lost out on five...ten...perhaps ten *thousand* more connections, all of which could have led to new business opportunities and revenue.

I now realize how crucial social media is to my company brand as well as my own. I've worked hard to grow my network since that time and successfully have by approximately five hundred percent. LinkedIn is now my network of choice and I get inbound business opportunities on a daily basis. While I still minimize the time I spend on these social networking sites, I do it in an efficient and productive way. I might spend five minutes here and there, but I know that I will never lose another two years.

Building Your Personal Brand

"Personal brands" have become extremely important for lifelong career success. Social media sites like LinkedIn, Twitter and Facebook have given everyone the opportunity to show off their expertise. Again, this is why it's so important to have a specific expertise, in a specific industry. Even if you ever lose your job, change careers or start a company, you will have your personal brand to fall back on. It stays with you always and make you valuable to other companies and people.

Earlier in the book, I mentioned that adding keywords to your resume will increase your chances of being found in a search. The same applies for your entire personal brand. You'll want to use the same or similar keywords throughout your online profiles. Add it to your LinkedIn, Twitter, Facebook, blog, and anywhere else you appear online to make it easier for search engines to find you.

It is essential to position yourself as a thought-leader. A thought-leader shares the best content in a specific niche, and creates new content and discussions. Providing new and innovative thoughts on specific topic will help you build your brand and give you more inbound opportunities. Recruiters are looking for thought leaders: people that take the time to share and write amazing articles. In fact, professionals who share articles or content with their network at least once a week are ten times more likely to be contacted by recruiter! And how could it not lead to a contact? Those who consistently share material make themselves known to recruiters, hiring managers, CEO's and other thought-leaders. For this reason, I urge you to complete and perfect your LinkedIn profile. LinkedIn is easily the most important social network for your online personal brand, so spend time making it great.

Content is important, but presenting yourself in a likable fashion is crucial as well. If you're overly-negative, mean or crude, your brand will be ruined. I advise you to always 'keep it classy.' Don't post pictures of yourself that you wouldn't want your mother to see, and don't post words that you can't take back. Remember, nothing can be truly deleted from the internet.

Get A Great LinkedIn Profile

Just like a résumé, most people will glance at your LinkedIn profile for fifteen to twenty seconds make their judgment of you. Your profile needs to be eye-catching and give viewers the correct impression of you. For example, look at your title. It is the first thing that people see; it needs to be impressive! You'll notice that mine has three parts to it:
"President at Culture Adapt | International Career Development Consultant | Professional Speaker"

Why the different parts?

It shows that I have a diverse skill set, multiple avenues of expertise, and it helps me appear in searches more often. The more keywords you can have throughout your profile, the more you will come up on in searches. If you are aspiring to be a social media marketing manager for a technology company, keywords like 'social media,' 'technology,' 'marketing manager,' 'Facebook' and 'Twitter' should be part of your title to make you more obvious a search result.

Next up is the 'Summary' section of your profile. Just like your résumé, it's at the very top of your profile and is your best chance to actually impress someone in that fifteen-second window. Hiring managers and recruiters are probably only going to look at your title and this part before deciding whether or not to contact you.

Keep in mind that you can also rearrange the sections of your LinkedIn profile, and place the most impressive ones at the top. Perhaps you've won a few awards: put those directly below your Summary. My preference at this stage in my career is to list my previous positions and then my 'recommendations,' which are really solidify my credibility. They show that I produce results, positively affect people's lives and provide instant social proof.

If you don't have any yet, you need to find recommenders for your own page. Recommendations from former employers, mentors, peers and clients will put you a notch above other candidates. How do you find recommenders?

By helping people!

Are you noticing a pattern yet? It's simple: the more recommendations you give, the more you will get. When you give someone a recommendation, they receive an e-mail. They will appreciate your support, and might give you one in return. If they don't, you can ask them directly via the LinkedIn recommendation system. Set a personal goal to give at least fifteen thoughtful recommendations.

You can do the same thing with 'Endorsements' section of your profile. LinkedIn members now have the ability to 'endorse' the skills of someone they know or have worked with. The more endorsements you have for different skills, the more easily a hiring manager or recruiter will see that you are an expert. Social proof is sometimes all you need to prove that you're the perfect candidate.

The last tip I have for perfecting your profile is to add websites to your profile. Many people don't think about this, but adding websites like your blog, your Twitter profile, and any other sites that show your expertise helps you appear in searches.

My LinkedIn Profile

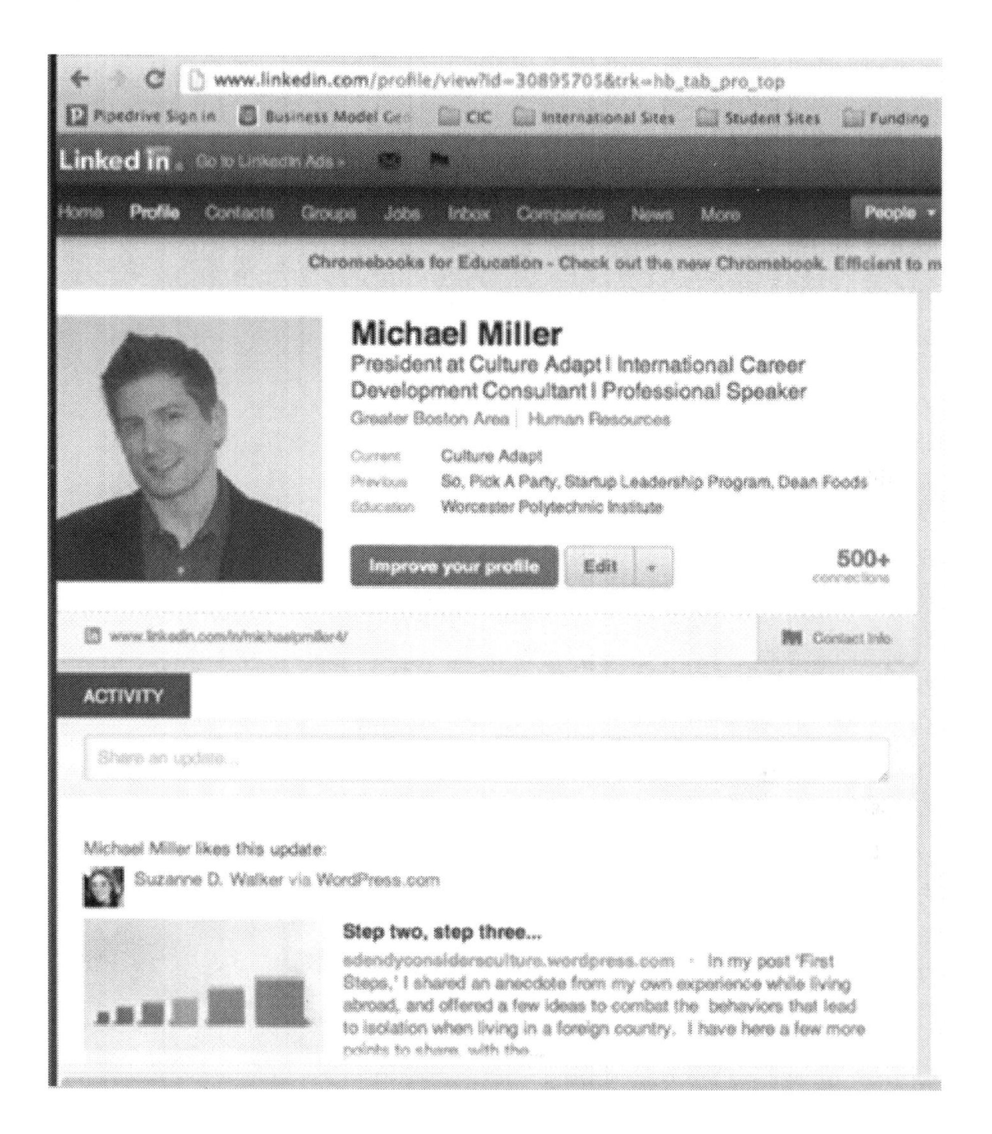

You may be thinking, "Ok, Michael, all of this advice sounds fine, but I need to SEE IT IN ACTION!"

Well, you're in luck. I'm going to walk you through my LinkedIn profile and explain why it's close-to-perfect (I can always improve). Let's take a look at the header first. You'll notice that my title has multiple parts, as I explained earlier. 'President at Culture

Adapt' shows both my company and position, 'International Career Development Consultant' defines more specifically what I do, and 'Professional Speaker' tells yet another specific skill I can provide. I do this because I want my name to appear at the top of the list when people search for 'career development' or 'international career development.'

You must also identify the industry in which you work. As you can see, I've chosen "Human Resources" because that's the field career development falls under. I'd also suggest that you personalize the link to your LinkedIn profile like I have (www.linkedin.com/in/michaelpmiller4). You'll also notice that I have "500+" connections. If you have 500-plus connections, this tells others that you probably have good networking and interpersonal skills. The goal should be at least 501 connections!

Below the header is my 'Activity Stream.' I try to make sure I always have useful or interesting updates in this section. I'm a thought-leader in international career development, so most of the things that I post are related to this field. If I can help people that view my profile without ever meeting them, they may try to help me too.

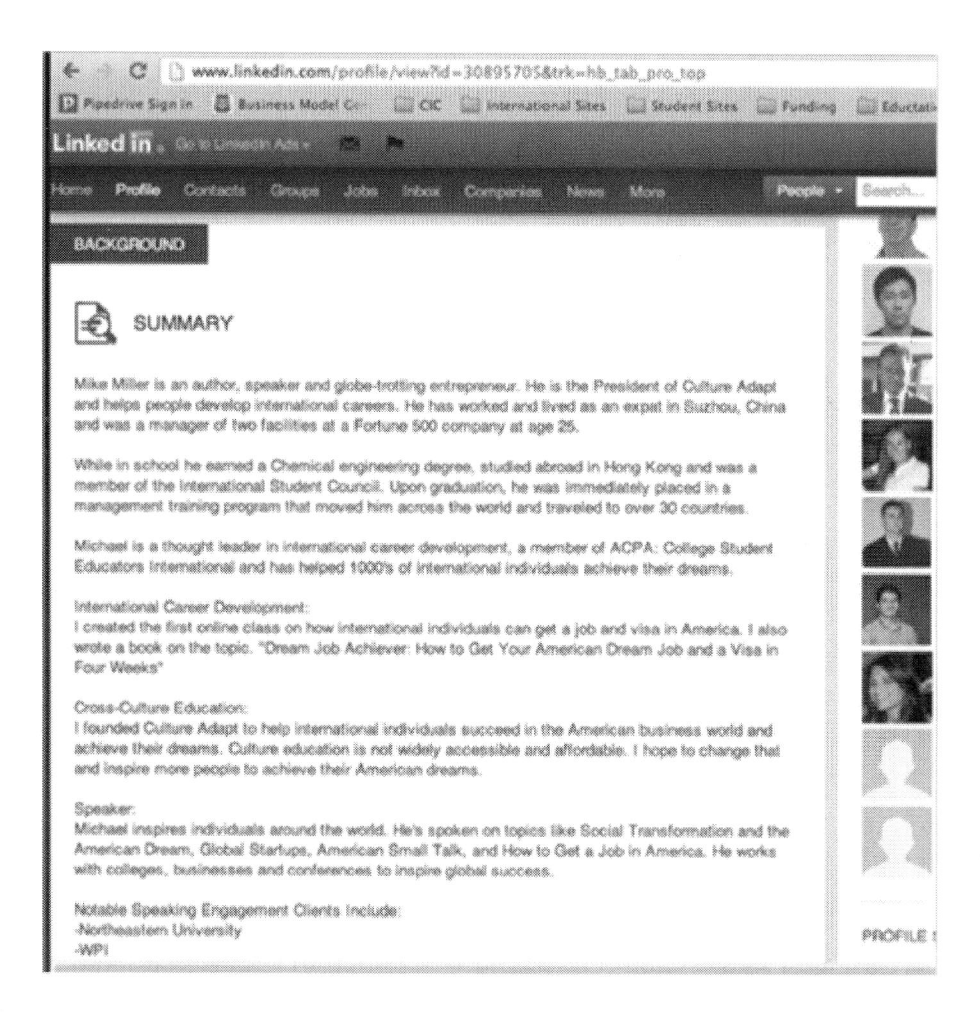

My "Summary" section tells a story of why I am an expert in my field. The first three sentences are interesting and impressive because I want to 'hook' the reader. It quickly explains what I've done and what makes me unique, citing a few accomplishments like my position as "manager of two facilities at a Fortune 500 company at age 25."

After I hook the reader, I continue to tell the story of my expertise. I show that I was an expatriate in Suzhou, China, earned a Chemical Engineering Degree, and travelled to over 30 countries. This may seem like I'm doing a little 'self-promotion'...because I am. In

America, this is normal, if not necessary. You have to show why you are different from everyone else.

Once I finish my story, I break down the different things that I do in an easy-to-read format. For example, under 'International Career Development,' I note that I created the first online class (Dream Job Achiever) to help internationals get a job and visa in America, and wrote a book on the subject.

Under "Speaker", I give some notable keynotes speeches and clients. I then list some of my key skills and finish my summary section off with actual proof of my work. You can add presentations, videos, papers, your blog or anything else. I have the slide deck and a video highlight of my workshop, "The Art of American Small Talk."

No one has to guess about the content of my work, and even if someone just glances at my summary, he will be able to tell that I am undoubtedly an expert.

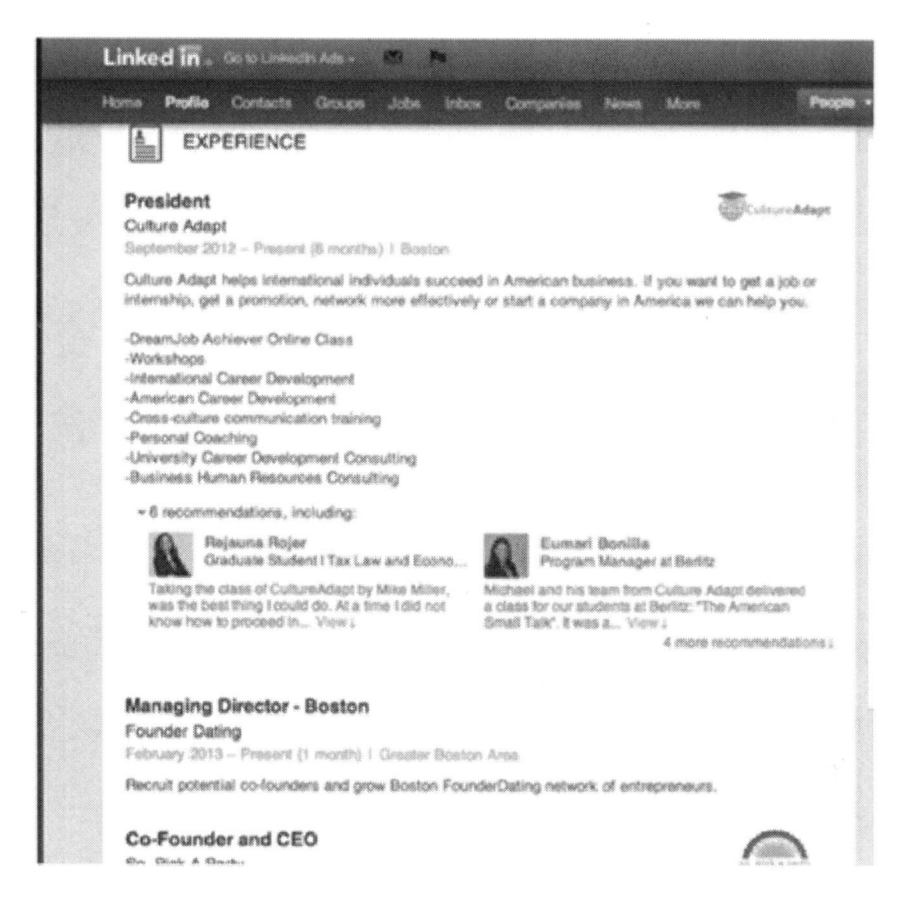

Next is my 'Experience' section. I have a short description of each position I've held and recommendations for each position. I think it's important to try to get a recommendation for each position, to strengthen your career history.

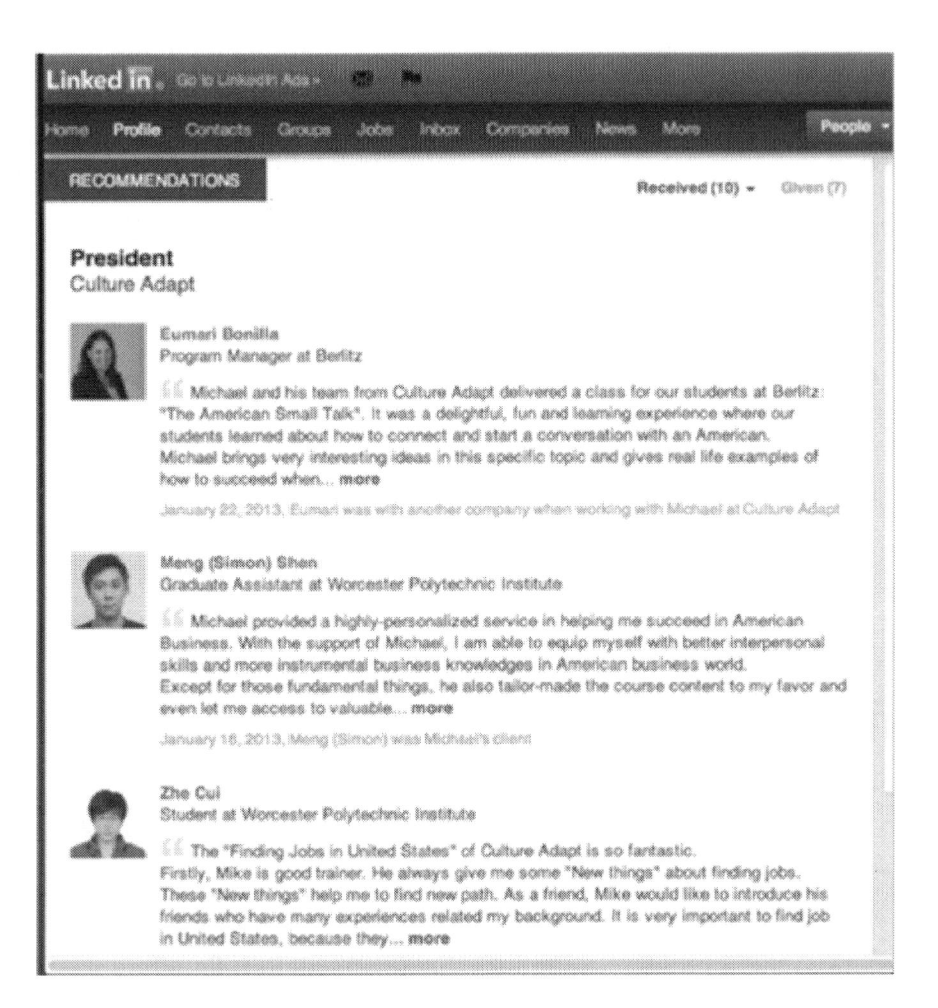

My 'Recommendations' section has opinions from previous students and business clients. I don't provide any guidance on what people should write but you can offer direction towards exactly what skills you'd like highlighted.

Next is my 'Skills & Expertise' section, and all the endorsements I have gained by endorsing others. You can delete skills that aren't relevant to your expertise, but I choose to keep all of them because I like to show my versatility. Does 'Process Improvement' directly relate to international career development? No. However, that skill does influence how I view and eliminate wasteful activity from the job search process.

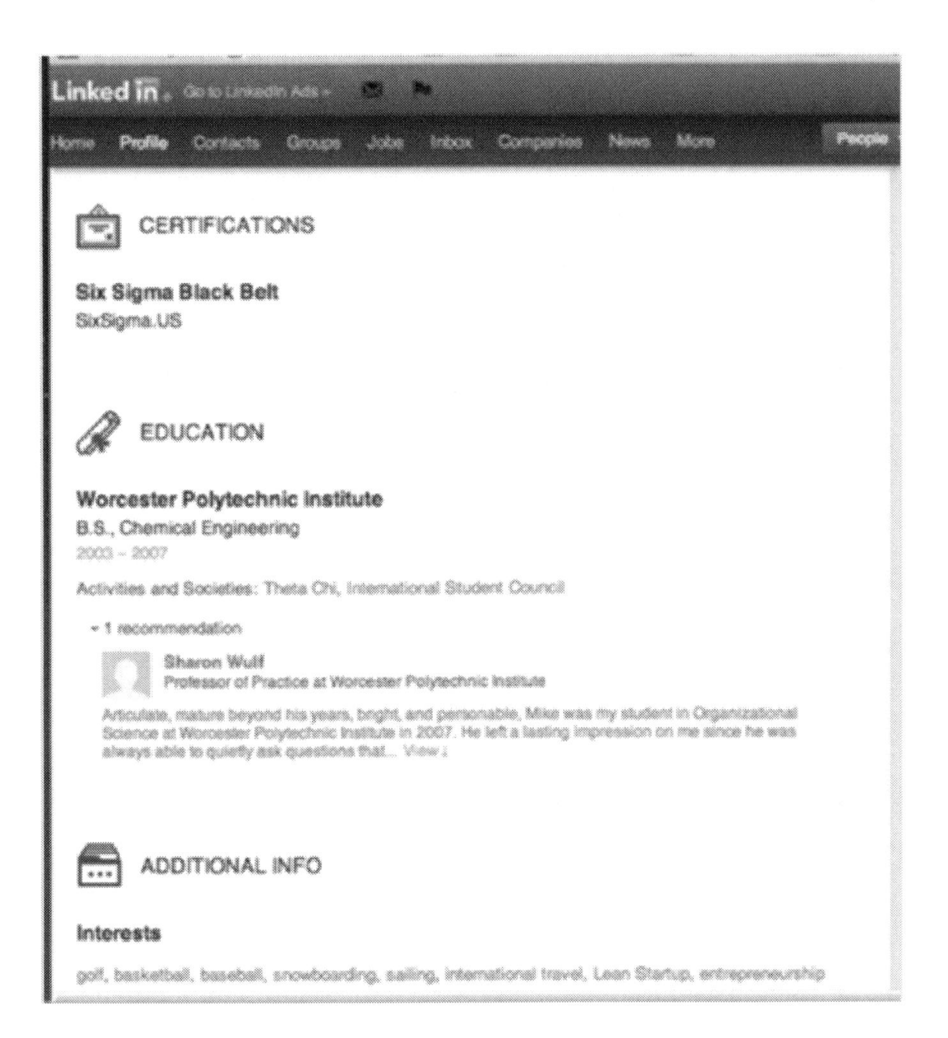

Next I list my certifications, including the Six Sigma Black Belt. I follow that with my education background and some random 'Interests.' I like people to know that I have interests outside of work, so I list out some things that may be a mutual interest like, basketball, snowboarding and international travel. Going back to the principles of small talk: this will allow others to find mutual interests and build a relationship with me more easily. Other parts of my profile that are not shown are 'Honors and Awards,' 'Groups' and 'Companies' that I follow. I am in 52 groups and follow companies that interest me or are in my field.

Use my profile to guide you in creating your own excellent profile and companies will be knocking down your door before you know it.

Three Clicks To Grow Your Connections By 100%

By networking, following up successfully and using my e-mail contact list, I have increased my LinkedIn connections by 600% over the last two years. For years, I didn't think it was important to grow my network because I didn't see an immediate benefit. When ever I changed jobs, I left hundreds of e-mail contacts with it. Some of those connections would now be amazing business opportunities but I have no idea how to get in contact with them. I'm going to save you from this same mistake and show you how to grow your LinkedIn network by 100% in three clicks of your mouse!

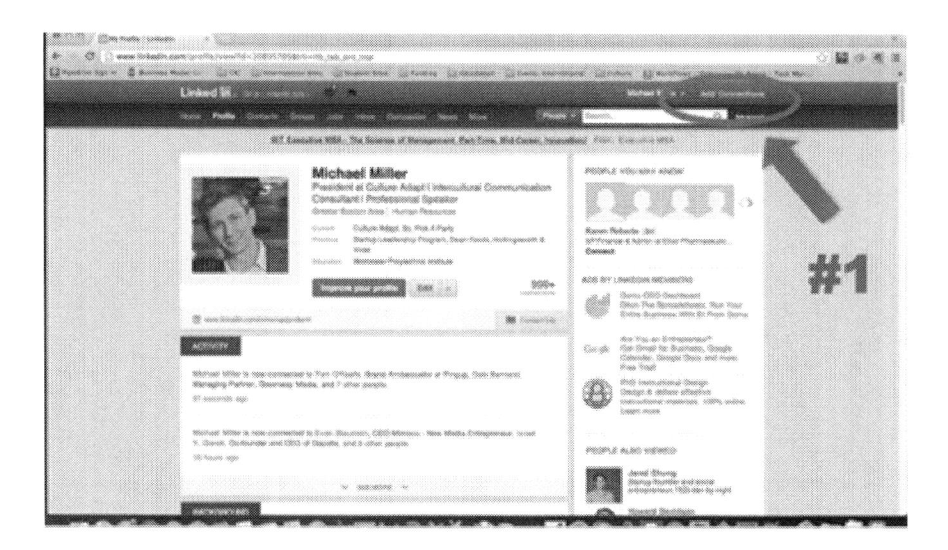

Click #1 - 'Add Connections'
In the upper right-hand corner of every page of LinkedIn, there is a green button that says 'Add Connections.' Click that button.

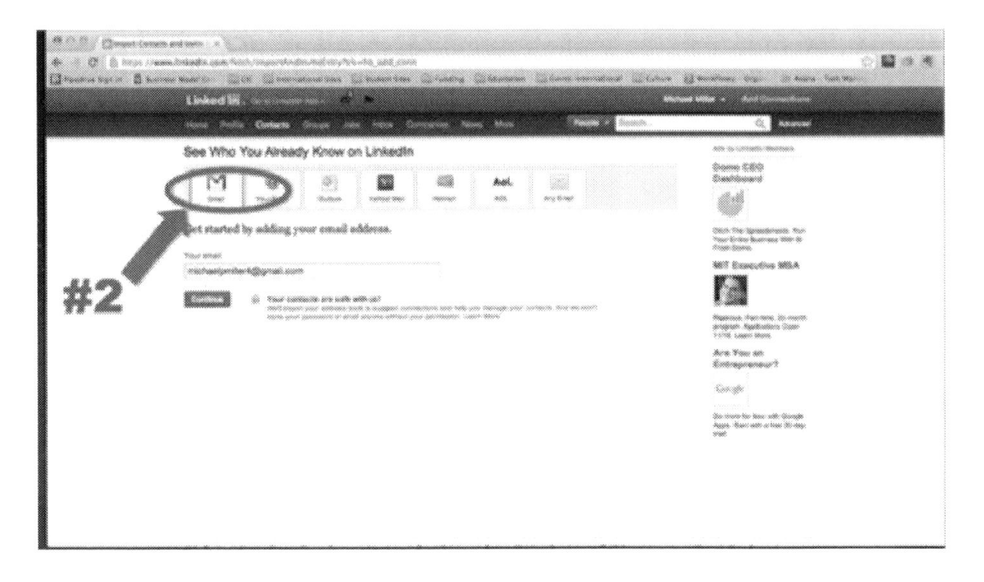

Click # 2- Choose Your Most Used Email
This will take you to a screen that will say 'See Who You Already Know on LinkedIn' and ask you to select an e-mail address. You can use your work e-mail, school e-mail, personal G-mail, Yahoo mail, or whatever other e-mail you use. Pick the one you use the most and enter your login info. I choose to use my work e-mail.

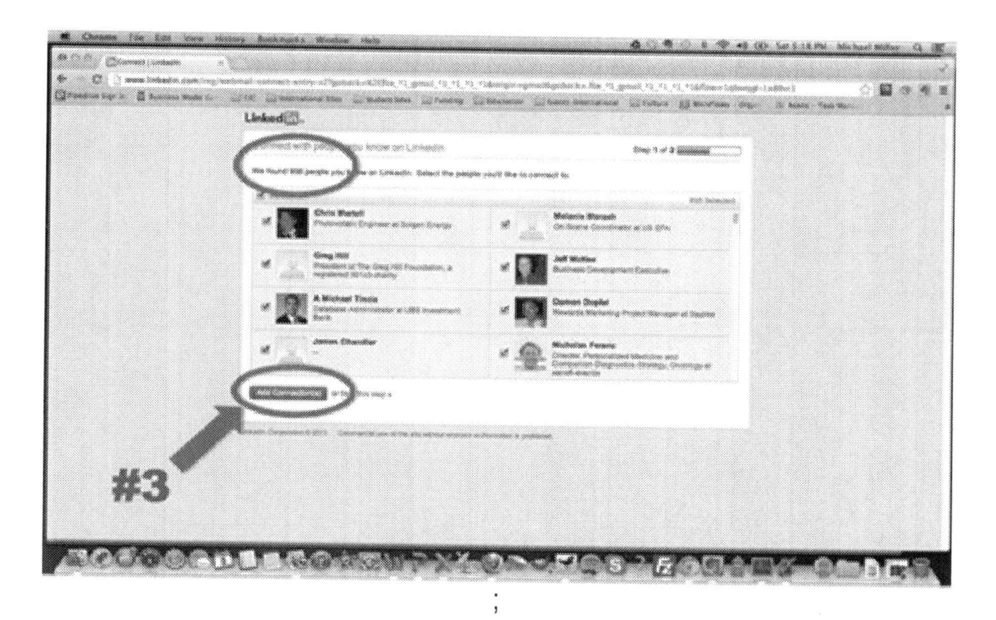

Click #3- 'Add Connections' again
LinkedIn pulls all your e-mail contacts and automatically finds their LinkedIn profile. Then you just click 'Add connections' and it will send a connection request to everyone. Some people are scared to add all their connections because they might not know some of them very well or at all. Don't worry about this. It's perfectly acceptable to request to connect with someone over LinkedIn if you have his or her e-mail. You can see in this example that I had 956 people that I wasn't already connected to. That was only after a couple weeks of e-mail too.

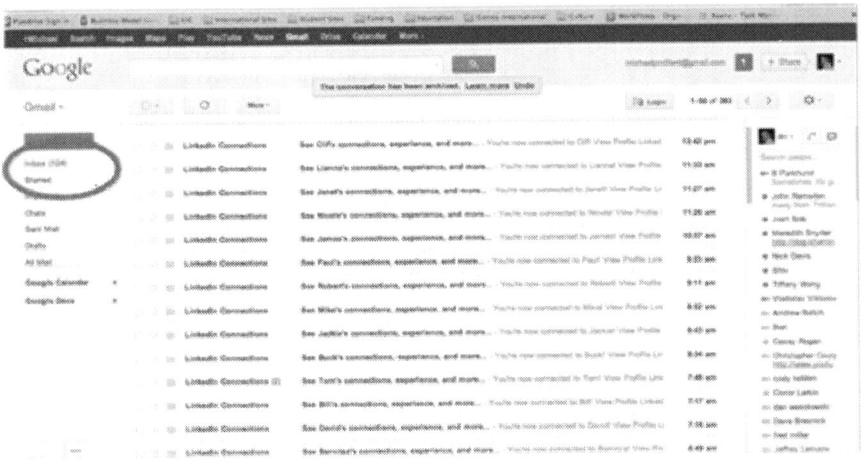

My Results 10 Hours Later – 124 New Connections!

Just ten hours after those three clicks, I already **124 new LinkedIn connections**! That's new people that can possibly connect me to job and business opportunities. Not to mention that it builds my 2nd and 3rd connections by thousands. If you recall, I told you how those 2nd and 3rd connections will lead to most of your opportunities. It should be clear why I strongly recommend that you repeat this process for all the e-mail contacts you have.

Five More Ways to Grow Your Network

It's important to try to grow your network every day. Here are five more ways to do just that.

- **Invite co-workers from past companies**
  Maybe you didn't get to know someone that well, or maybe you didn't even meet but the former co-worker is much more likely to accept your request simply because you two worked at the same place. Then, you can reach out and connect further still to that person's connections.

- **Invite classmates from past and/or present school**
  Again, it's much easier to connect with someone if you have a common company, school, or group. Feel free to connect with anyone on that mutual connection.

- **Join More Groups and invite members**
  If you're not in fifty-two groups, find and join fifty-two targeted groups. Then invite other members of that group to connect with you.

- **Join the LinkedIn Group 'International Career Development'**
  I personally run this largest international career development group on LinkedIn. You can make many great connections in it.

- **Connect with LinkedIn 'LION' or open networking groups**
  The LinkedIn 'LION' is somewhat of a secret. It is a special term that professionals use for themselves if they are 'open networkers,' meaning they will connect with absolutely anyone. These LIONs are constantly trying to grow their network because they realize it will help them in the long run. There are many LinkedIn LION groups as well as multiple websites where you can connect with other LIONs. Along with the groups and websites, you can always type the word LION into the LinkedIn advanced search and it will find people with that keyword in their profile. Again, you might not personally know these people but they could provide a connection to people at one of your dream companies.

Questions & Actions

Should I have the LinkedIn title, 'looking for new opportunity'?

I personally don't like it. I think it can seem a little desperate and doesn't display your personal value. If you're out meeting the right people like you are supposed to do, they will know you're looking. You will get better results if you have multiple *specific* parts to your title. For example, if you are an aspiring tax consultant, a graduate student and the president of a charitable organization, your title should be "President at (organization) | Tax Consultant | Graduate Student."

Is it okay to call people I have e-mailed and but who never replied?
Yes, it's fine. Maybe your follow-up e-mail was a little off but you can always fix that situation. Call them and quickly grab their attention. Focus on helping and they will be a lot more open to talking to you.

How do I efficiently manage all my social media profiles?
I use a tool called Hootsuite. Hootsuite allows you to post one update to all of your social media profiles at one time. It also allows you to schedule your posts in advance! I usually set aside an hour at the beginning of the week and schedule the entire weeks worth of posts for my Facebook pages, Twitter accounts, LinkedIn profile, and LinkedIn Group. It's much more time effective and simplifies my social network life. I typically schedule three to five Facebook posts/day, five to ten tweets/day, and one to two LinkedIn posts/day. You don't need to post much at all, even if you're running a company.

Personal Challenge
Get 30 Twitter Followers (2 days)

If you don't have a Twitter account, start one and get thirty people to 'follow' you. If you already have an account, get thirty more people to follow you. I'd also like you to try to get someone famous to reply to one of your tweets. By 'someone famous,' I mean famous in your industry or the business world. Try starting discussions by sharing useful articles, quotes or thoughtful comments. It will be easier than you think and will be important to your business career down the road. You can even follow me (@mmiller1222) and my company (@cultureadapt) and probably follow you back.

Tools & Resources

Hootsuite.com - A great way to manage all your social media profiles at once.

Twitter.com – Micro blogging site with over 140 million users worldwide.

Dream Job Achiever (www.cultureadapt.com/dreamjobachiever) - My online class that covers ever topic in this book and more. Hours of videos, action guides, audio interviews and more scripts to help you succeed.

Part 4:
Bullseye

"Success is getting what you want. Happiness is wanting what you get. – *Dale Carnegie*

Chapter 12 - Ace The Interview

"Knowledge speaks, but wisdom listens." - *Jimi Hendrix*

"Think twice before you speak, because your words and influence will plant the seed of either success or failure in the mind of another." - *Napoleon Hill*

Weakness Becomes Strength

"You should take my class because I give all my students A's. That's what's important right?" The older professor smiled as he said this to Asie.

They were sitting in the waiting room before one of the biggest moments of Asie's life: a final interview at one of her dream companies, PwC. She was confused as to why there was a professor in the waiting room with her and the other candidates, and taken aback by his conversational tone. By the time the topic of studies had arisen, they had been chatting for a good while. Finally it came up that Asie was still at a university, getting her Master's of Science in Accounting. At this point, the professor made his sly suggestion.

Being the strong, opinionated person she is, Asie quickly expressed her disagreement. "No, that's not what's important. The acquisition of knowledge, skills and real-life application are what truly matter in a class."

The professor was clearly surprised by her willingness to contradict him, but smiled and said, "Good answer." Little did Asie, know PwC had planted the professor character to judge candidates *prior* to their actual interviews. This creative test didn't slow her down a bit and before she knew it, Asie was called into the interview room.

Just months before, Asie had identified interviewing as a skill she needed to improve. She knew that her confidence was low because her heavy accent often masked her otherwise flawless English, and she didn't know the complex terminology of business English. She decided to take action and try to improve. She bought books on business English, and watched YouTube tutorial videos on accent reduction. She would record her voice and play it back over and over again. Even when practicing a mere fifteen minutes a day, Asie began to notice improvement.

Her new business vocabulary allowed her to express herself in the way she was accustomed to and her accent reduction allowed others to understand her more easily. Suddenly, she was more confident in both business and social settings (so confident that she had no problem walking up to campus recruiters and telling them why she was a great candidate)! Networking introductions like these ultimately led to interviews at three of "The Big Four."

Even though she knew that her language skills had improved, she was still going to face many cultural differences during the interview process. Naturally, the types of questions she'd be asked, the expectations of the company, and the 'right' kind of answers would all differ from an interview in her native Bulgaria. To prepare, she researched online and asked current employees during informational interviews. From this research, she developed a list of questions that she would likely be asked. She then carefully thought out her own answers, wrote them down and practiced them out loud to mentally prepare herself for the big days. She also researched the company to give her the ability to strike up discussions on current, real-world issues the company and its employees might be facing. By the day of the interview, she had done everything she could to prepare herself.

At last, Asie was sitting in the PwC office. She still couldn't get over how relaxed and laid back the American interview process was. More than anything, it emphasized the ability to connect with other people and communicate effectively. Company recruiters and employees had told her, "We can teach you everything. We are just looking for good interpersonal skills and a company culture fit."

In this environment, Asie used her small talk skills like a pro, building bridges on common interests and sharing personal stories that intrigued and entertained. Throughout the interview she continued to build the relationship and seal the deal. She gave compliments and asked tough questions. The interviewer was pleasantly surprised and when the interview ended, the partner smiled and told her she was great!

All three of the companies had a similar two round interview process. The first round took place with a single manager, while the second round consisted of three different morning interviews and a final lunch interview. She used her newly acquired skills like a master and completed each with a sense of confidence.

Just one week after the interviews completed, she got the call she'd been waiting for: "Hi Asie. We want to let you know that you got the job."

"Yes!" She let out a cry of excitement, thinking *how it could get any better*? The next day another company called, and then another. Asie had received three job offers in a one-week period while many of her fellow classmates, both international and American, didn't even get a single interview. The time she spent turning her weaknesses into strengths and preparing for an American-style interview had paid off. Her H-1B visa and job at PwC were in hand.

14 Most Common Interview Mistakes

You can be great at every part of the American job search process, but if you don't learn how to interview well, you will never get your dream job. You are facing many cultural differences, such as appearance, questions and giving acceptable answers. To make sure that you ace every single interview (and there will be plenty, if you follow the steps I've laid out), I'm going to share with you the most common mistakes that people make during an interview.

- **Answering a phone call or text**
  Leave your cell phone on silent and *never* pull out of your pocket. Nothing is ruder than using a phone during an interview.

- **Dressing inappropriately**
  Being underdressed or wearing revealing, wild or unprofessional clothing will make a bad impression.

- **Appearing disinterested**
  If during the interview you are spacing out, not actively listening, looking out the window, or giving an impression of disinterest, your interview will notice, and be turned off.

- **Appearing arrogant**
  You want to be confident, but not arrogant. There is a distinct difference, and you must learn to recognize it. Keep in mind that the interviewer has a higher position at this point, already being a working member of the company. You do not know everything there is to know, so try to be a little modest.

- **Chewing gum**
  Leave the gum at home or throw it out before you enter the interview. You do want to have good breath, but it's considered rude (and obnoxious) to chew gum while talking.

- **Not providing specific questions**
  If you have not done your homework and do not have questions specifically about the company or position, it will appear as if you don't care.

- **Not asking *good* questions**
  Not all questions are made equal. There are well-thought out questions, and then there are poor questions like, "Do I have to stay until five p.m. every day?" Make sure you avoid these small, common-sense questions so as not to waste time.

- **Speaking negatively about a previous employer**
  Any negativity in general is bad for an interview, but this mistake is especially bad. As soon as an interviewee speaks negatively about a former employer, the interview is over. Even if you do have a legitimate claim against a former employer, bringing such grievances up in front of others is tactless, disrespectful of your former boss, and shows poor interpersonal skills.

- **Hugging interviewer**
  While this may be acceptable in some cultures, it is not appropriate in America. A firm handshake is the way to go.

- **Wearing a hat**
  Hats are never acceptable for interviews, nor most business environments.

- **Seeming desperate**
  Even if you are desperate, don't let it show. This reveals a lack of confidence and makes you appear less valuable to the interviewer.

- **Talking about relationships or love life**
  Leave your personal relationships at the door. It's considered unprofessional to speak about your love life in an interview.

- **Never smiling**
  Make sure you smile! Employers want to hire someone who is sociable and easy to get along with.

- **One-word answers**
  Make sure that you are adding value to the conversation and saying more than just 'yes' and 'no.' This is your opportunity to share yourself with the interview! Don't waste that chance.

Cultural Barriers To Interview Success

Going into an interview without educating yourself on cultural differences is like flying a plane blindfolded: not a wise decision. Luckily, you are clever enough to prepare yourself, and become aware of the differences you will face. You will notice that the differences I mention in American interview culture relate directly back to Hofstede's cultural dimensions.

Self-promotion
I have mentioned this a few times throughout the book but I reiterate: you need to be willing to promote yourself and your skills. In some countries it may be considered rude behavior, but in America it is necessary to tell interviewers why you are great and different from other candidates. If you are not comfortable doing this or are worried that you will appear arrogant, you need to practice with a mentor.

Directness
Americans are very direct, so don't ask vague questions or give long drawn-out answers. At times it may seem a little cold or awkward but don't get offended. Work on getting right to the point, being concise, and not wasting anyone's time.

Self-disclosure

While it is not acceptable to share your love life, it is very acceptable to disclose other parts of your personal life like your hobbies, what you like to do for fun on weekends, places you've traveled, etc. In fact, if you avoid disclosing personal information, you will appear cold and aloof. Think back to the list of small talk topics to avoid, and keep these same topics out of interviews. Meanwhile, show off your personality and the amazing interpersonal skills you have worked hard to improve.

Informality

Sometimes international individuals are confused by the informality of American interviews. Many interviews are similar to a conversation, so make sure you build a relationship.

Career Self-Awareness

In America, it is respected and important to know what you want to do with your career. This book should be helping you build your career self-awareness. You should be trying to get a job in a field you are excited and passionate about! At some point during most interviews, you will be asked, "Where do you see yourself in five years?" Knowing the answer to that question will be hugely beneficial.

Punctuality

In other countries it can be common to show up late for meetings or interviews. In America, you need to be five to fifteen minutes early. If you are late, companies may even cancel the interview! Arriving early shows employers that you are organized, punctual and responsible.

I suggest five to fifteen minutes because if you are there thirty minutes early, that can actually give a wrong impression. You may appear desperate or unable to schedule your day effectively. A trick that I like to do is to arrive to the area a half hour to an hour ahead of time, and sit in a nearby coffee shop until it is time to walk in.

Individual equity

Individualism is a key part of American culture. Having your own thoughts and dreams is admired. For this reason, interviewers will appreciate that you have your own aspirations and are driven to achieve them. Don't be scared to share them as long as they are in line with the job you are interviewing for.

Preparedness

Preparing for an interview is extremely important. If you walk into an interview without researching the company and having specific questions to ask, it will appear as if you don't care. You must show your enthusiasm for the company and position. Personally, I don't think you can ever be over-prepared.

8 Ways To Impress Your Interviewer

Now that you now everything to avoid and common cultural barriers, it's time to learn how to really impress people. It's time to show the world why you're such an amazing person.

Stay energetic

Throughout the interview stay excited and happy: you are about to get your dream job! High-energy people typically have a higher chance of success.

Admit your ignorance

If you are asked a question that you don't know the answer to, it's better to admit it than try to make something up. Interviewers are trained to quickly realize when you are trying to trick them. They will respect you for admitting when you are lost. Just say something like, "I'm not really familiar with that. Could you please tell me a little bit more about it?"

Avoid interrupting

When the interviewer is talking, do not interrupt them. You have to show that you can be a good listener. If you find yourself interrupting them several times throughout the interview, slow down, try to relax and wait for them to finish talking. A pause is better than an interruption.

Treat the interviewer like the decision-maker

This is a cool trick that I like to use in interviews and business meetings. Basically, you just have to treat anyone that is interviewing you like they are the most important person in the company. Act like they can hand you the job. This will make them feel more powerful, and they will like you for it. Ask them what kind of person they are looking to hire, what their perfect candidate is like, and where they think the company is succeeding.

Use specific experiences

When I interview, most of my answers start with stories from my life. Specific work, project, team, and personal experiences are the most powerful things you can use. Being able to tell these stories will help others get to know you and understand why you are a perfect fit.

Don't Overdo it

Don't put on a lot of perfume or cologne, as it will be distracting and unpleasant. Different people have different smell tolerances so don't overdo it. Take a shower before the interview, use deodorant and try to smell as "normal" as possible.

Be memorable

As I've said that throughout book, you want to be memorable. Being yourself, passionate, outgoing or an expert in your field can make you memorable. Your creative and unique stories and experiences will help people remember you too. Use your new small talk skills to build that relationship quickly!

Research

You must know the current state of a company, recent important events and possibly their future goals. You need to try to find specific problems that you can help solve. You can search for articles, press releases and follow the company on LinkedIn, Twitter and Facebook. You can also ask other people that follow the company, "Why do you like this company?"

You can also research your interviewers if you get their names beforehand. Look them up on Google and LinkedIn and see what information you can find. If you went to the same school, lived in the same city or have mutual interests, make sure to bring it up during the interview.

Preparing Like A Pro

A lot of people ask me, "Michael, how do you prepare for an interview?"

My method is fairly simple but was crucial to my success. First, I would create a list of questions that I would possibly be asked during the interview. My online research, informational interviews and mentors were the sources of those questions. It was a great exercise because it got me thinking about the types of questions that my target company would ask and what they might find important.

Once I had a decent list (forty to fifty questions), I would write down answers for each of them. I made sure that all my answers were specific and cited past experiences. This does take a while to do, but it was always worth it. It helps me remember my answers, and makes interviewing much easier. I was more confident, answered questions faster and seemed really sharp. People get nervous in interviews and when you're nervous, it's harder to remember things. By writing your answers down, you limit the chances that your mind will draw a blank

I would also have mentors and peers mock-interview me for practice. I'd have them critique my answers, appearance, body language, and interpersonal skills throughout. The day of the interview, I'd review my notes, say some answers in front of a mirror, and listen to some high-energy techno-music before heading in, to ensure I was high energy.

Look The Part

Part of your social transformation has to do with appearing like the social status you are striving to achieve. If you're trying to be a financial analyst, mimic that certain appearance standard. If you want to be an executive, notice that different standard. Different companies have different standards as well. This is why your appearance is so important when trying to ace an interview.

Of course, you want to shower in the morning, be well groomed, shaven, have clean teeth, clean-cut hairstyle and ironed clothes. Again, don't chew gum or smoke before an interview. Smoking is really frowned upon by some Americans, so it's best to avoid smelling of smoke. You can also ask human resources at the company if the dress is "business casual" or "business professional" (typically a full suit).

When choosing an outfit, make sure it's not too bold or flashy (leave the bright orange shoes and neon-pink necklace at home). You can however, wear a 'conversation piece': something unique or interesting that will attract attention. This piece should be eye-catching, and you can then tell the story behind it. This will intrigue and impress others. It could be something like a watch, ring, necklace or tie; regardless, it will show your confidence and individuality.

Still need more direction? Here are some fashion tips for both men and women that will work for most interviews.

Men's Interview Attire

- Suit (solid color – navy, black or dark grey)
- Long-sleeve colored shirt (white or coordinated with suit)
- Leather belt
- Sharp tie
- Dark socks
- Shined leather shoes
- Watch personalized to your style
- Neatly trimmed fingernails
- Portfolio or briefcase (*no* backpacks)

Women's Interview Attire

- Suit (solid color – navy, black or dark grey)
- Pantsuit or tailored dress with coat also work
- Suit skirt long enough to sit down comfortably (can opt for pants too)

- Coordinated blouse
- Mid-heeled shoes
- Limited jewelry (make sure it's not cheap)
- Professional hairstyle
- Neutral pantyhose
- Manicured clean nails (no bright yellow nail polish, for example)
- Portfolio or briefcase (*no* backpacks)

Common Questions You'll Hear

Really quickly we'll go through some of the common questions that you will hear in an interview.

"Why do you want this job?"
You've already spent a lot of time narrowing down the answer to this question for yourself, so now you should be able to answer this question easily.

"Why should I hire you for this job?"
This goes back to self-promotion: if you've completed the Career Blueprint, you know the answer to this question.

"What are your strengths and weaknesses?"
Again, you've already done this. You should be noticing how this book has already prepared you for your interview moment.

"Tell me about a time when..."
This is a common way to start a question in an interview. They can ask you about a time you were on a difficult team, completed a project successfully, made a mistake, etc. If you've prepared properly and have a bunch of stories written down, these kinds of questions won't be a problem.

"Tell me about your experience at..."
This question could be about your previous company or previous school. For example, if I was asked "Tell me about your experience at Hollingsworth & Vose," I'd explain what I worked on, what I enjoyed there, and my results. You need to stay positive no matter what, and focus on measurable results.

"What salary range are you looking for?"
I love this question. Typically it will not hurt you, but it could. That's why I like to gracefully avoid the question. I never discussed salary until I had the job offer in hand. I would say something like, "I'd really rather discuss salary when we're at that stage and you're ready to hire me."

You're saying, "hire me," without actually saying it. That displaying your value!

Tougher Questions

Companies need employees that can think on their feet and outside the box. This is why riddles and problem-solving questions have become more popular during interviews. You need to be prepared to answer these questions; otherwise you may freeze up when you are faced with one.

These are a few tough questions to get you started.

"On a scale of one to ten, how *weird* are you?"
How would you answer that? You have to get creative and give a well thought-out answer. One thing I'd suggest is reading the interviewer, and judging how laid back they are. If they seem to be more relaxed, you can joke, "Well I'm probably a ten! I have a lot of

odd quirks, but that's what makes me unique." A safer option would be saying, "I'm a five: just about as weird as everyone else."

"How many basketballs can you fit in this room?"
This is a great example of a problem-solving question. You have to think about the circumference of a basketball, the average area one takes up, the approximate area of the room and then calculate it out from there.

"How many ridges are there around a quarter?"
Do you have a quarter in your pocket? Do they have one? Maybe the secretary does?

"An apple costs twenty cents, an orange costs forty cents, and a grapefruit costs sixty cents. How much is a pear?"
Are you missing information? What questions can you ask? If you can't get any more information how would you price a pear based on what you know?

"How do you weigh an elephant without using a weigh machine?"
Have it sit on a car?

"What do wood and alcohol have in common?"
Both have hit me hard before.

These are some great ones to practice on but find more online. Improving your problem-solving skills and building your critical thinking capabilities will help you throughout your career.

Interview Day Checklist

This is a quick ten-point checklist that you can bring with you the day of your interview. Having this reminder will help you relax and ace it!

1. Shower
2. Be early
3. Bring resume copies (ten to fifteen copies)
4. Greet with confidence (remember names)
5. Maintain high-energy
6. Display value
7. Use strong body language
8. Ask intelligent questions
9. Avoid salary questions
10. Thank interviewer, shake hands at end of interview

Professional Video Interviews

Video interviews are becoming more popular everywhere, especially for global companies. It's more cost and time effective for everyone. This is why you must start learning how to conduct a professional video interview and if you live outside the country, you need to learn how to do this today! These are some tips to make your video interview look very professional without spending much money.

Background: Make sure whatever is behind you is professional. A blank colored wall, bookshelf, or office setting works well. You want to avoid bedrooms, bathrooms, crowded areas or anything that could give a future employer the wrong impression.

Lighting: Bring all your lamps to the video area and aim them on yourself to enable viewers to see you more clearly. You'd be surprised how much light it actually takes to give a clear picture.

High definition webcam: You can buy a high definition camera off of Amazon.com for $30-$100.

Appropriate Dress: Dress just like you would for an in-person interview.

Control noise: Make sure that there is no background noise. Don't try to do an interview in a coffee shop or with people talking in the room next to you. It's distracting and unprofessional.

Test connection speed: If your connection speed is low it could ruin the audio and video quality of the interview. Check your connection speed using speedtest.net.

Look at camera, not screen: This is the most common mistake that people make. They look at the face of the interviewer instead of the camera. This makes it appear as if you aren't paying attention or looking down constantly. Look *into* the camera.

Practice: Skype and Google Hangout are two free and commonly-used video interview software. Have mock-interviews with peers and mentors, using these programs.

Be yourself: If you have a good sense of humor, are high-energy or normally use a lot of body language in conversations… do the same over video. Let your personality shine on screen.

A video interview is never easy but by following these tips you will succeed!

Questions & Actions

What types of interviews are there in America?
There are many different types of interviews in America: behavioral based, work sample, case study, luncheon, group and panel interviews, to name a few. Really, it depends on the industry you hope to enter, so you will need to do your own research. Whatever the type of interview, however, you will face similar questions and be held to the same standards.

Also, large companies tend to be have formal interview processes, while many start-ups or small companies have informal ones. In your online research, you might be able to find case studies of people that have interviewed at that company before. If you've met people at the company, you will already have a good sense of that company culture.

In my culture, talking with your hands and being expressive with your face is common. What about America?
Yes, it's very common to talk with hand gestures and make expressions. You'll notice some people are more expressive than others, but I believe that are more expressive tend to have better interpersonal skills. Continue to be expressive and passionate, and it will benefit you throughout your entire life.

How can I show more confidence?
Amy Cuddy performed research at Harvard Business School which revealed that holding your body in a "high-power" pose for as little as two minutes stimulates higher levels of testosterone —the hormone linked to dominance—and lower levels of cortisol, a stress hormone. You want that testosterone to give you an advantage during an interview!

What is a "high power" pose? An example would be leaning back in a chair with your hands behind your head, and the feet up on the desk. Another is called "pride", which is just throwing your arms out in joy! Do either of these poses before going to the interview to get an increased sensation of power and higher tolerance of risk. Try one of those poses right now and notice the difference.

Nonverbals govern how we think and feel about ourselves so it's extremely important that you work on this. All successful business leaders know how to use the power of body language to their advantage. [1]

What services can I use to reduce my accent?

You can search online for accent reduction classes in your area or search YouTube to find free accent reduction practice videos. You can also use a company called LessAccent (www.lessaccent.com).

Chapter 13 - Negotiate The Offer

"Negotiating is not something to be avoided or feared - it's an everyday part of life." - *Leigh Steinberg*

40% Salary Increase in 20 minutes

"We'd like to offer you the position Michael. We think you're a great fit and will really contribute a lot to the company. That's why we're willing start you at..."

Dean Foods had decided that despite being twenty-five years old, I was the right person for the job. I was thrilled, but knew that I couldn't show it. Even after I was offered a twenty-five percent salary increase from the position I currently held, I needed to maintain my 'poker face.' While most people would be happy such an offer, I knew that I deserved and could make more. I knew exactly what I was worth.

"That's great. I will have to think about this and get back to you," I replied confidently. "I really like my current position, but think this would be a great challenge and I could really help save a lot of money."

We continued the discussion somewhat, and all the while he tried to get me to commit. I didn't give in, instead pushing the negotiation off to a later phone call. It was difficult for me to do this because I *was* ready to leave my previous job. I was ready for bigger and better things, and knew that I was going to take this job. In spite of this, I acted like the decision was not made in my mind, because this would give me leverage in negotiations. No one else knew the thoughts going through my mind, my current salary or how badly I wanted the job.

Three days later, I emailed to schedule the next negotiation call. The very next day, the phone rang. I picked it up and knew that the Dean Foods hiring manager was going to be on the other line.

"Hi Michael. So did you have some time to think about the offer?"

This was my one chance to get the salary raise.

"Yes, I've thought about it and I did some research on my salary you offered me and think it's a little low. The average for this position is about $20,000 more than you first offer. I think that I will easily contribute ten times that in the first year," I said, trying to hide my nervousness. "In my last company, I saved roughly $500,000 in the last six months alone. Each of your plants is about four times the size of my current facility and I will be managing TWO. And these are two of your largest plants in the country."

This information I had gathered online and with informational interviews. It was clear that the hiring manager was surprised. He responded, "Oh, Michael…that might be a problem because we have different pay scales and... and.. you only have a couple years of experience."

"Yes, I know but I want to focus on the impact that I'm going to have on this company. It has nothing to do with my years of experience or the pay scale the position is in. I think what I asked for is fair." I replied, gaining confidence. "I'd also like to ask for four weeks of vacation as that seems to be average for this type of position."

I told him this to give him an 'out,' or a way to negotiate with something less important than my original salary request. I knew that hiring managers have trained negotiation skills, and if I didn't give him an 'out,' he'd be forced to lower my salary.

"That's asking a lot but let me get back to you," he said quickly.

He called back a day later, and we negotiated a little more before reaching an agreement. In the end my negotiations resulted in a forty percent salary increase and three weeks of paid vacation (the same amount as someone that had been with the company for 10 years).

"I'll be honest with you" he said in a quiet voice, "no one else in your position is making this much."

I smiled and replied, "That's fine. I think I'll be worth it."

The Art of Negotiation

Negotiation is an art, just like small talk. First you must educate yourself, then practice and improve. You need to overcome your fears of being rejected and confidently ask for more. To feel confident in your requests, you need statistics and metrics that validate your negotiable points. Many people don't understand the negotiation process because they don't educate themselves on the topic. The believe the stories told by someone, who heard it from someone who heard it from someone else. To help you understand it all, I'm going to debunk some myths about job negotiations that you may have heard.

Myth 1 - You may lose the job if you ask for a salary increase

You will never lose your job opportunity by asking for a salary increase. By the time you are given the offer, the company has a spent a lot of time and energy deciding on the perfect candidate. They have interviewed many people and had countless meetings before giving you that congratulatory phone call.

Hiring managers actually prepare for and expect you to ask for a salary increase. If you don't, they are going to be happily surprised, because it's one less task for them. Be certain you have done your research on average salaries for that position and don't ask for something completely ridiculous. Still, the worst that will happen is that they say "NO" to your request.

Myth 2 - Your position is trapped in a pay scale

Hiring managers always tell you that they must abide by certain 'rules' when setting a salary. These rules usually involve something called pay scales (a hierarchy of wage levels, typically varying according to job title, salary or length of service). The hiring manager will say that he or she has 'no control' over the situation, because every employee has to fit into the existing pay scale.

Don't believe this. If a company *really* wants you and you can help them accomplish their goals, they will be willing to pay. Tell them you will be the exception to the rule, and that you should be able to move into a higher pay scale because of what you will provide for the company.

Myth 3 - You need more years of experience to get paid more
There are thousands of twenty-something entrepreneurs making millions of dollars every year. You may not be starting your own company, but you can have just as big of an impact on a business. If you can prove that you will make a company more money, you can justify their paying you more—regardless of your age or experience. Salary has little to do with years in the field, and everything to do with the results you produce.

Myth 4 - Hiring managers are your friend
It's a very simple equation: salary/employee value = acquisition cost. The hiring manager's job is to get the best talent possible for the least amount of money. They will even have job assessment on this, so don't think for a *second* that they have your best interests in mind. Remember that people are constantly thinking about themselves and how to achieve *their own* career goals.

The Hiring Game

You must understand the psychology of a hiring manager before you can successfully negotiate with him or her. You need to know how and why they work. To do this, imagine salary negotiation like a game. While it's a rare, important instant in your life, the person you're negotiating with does it on a weekly basis. They are competing against you in a game which they practice routinely, with all of their existing skills and strategy.

They will start you as low as possible, with a repertoire of things to say to throw you off course, such as: "I'm your friend here," "Let me check with my boss," "Well, the economy is bad so..." or "There's just no way we could go any higher."

Don't fall for these. Stay focused on your goal and know your value. Now it's your job to be persuasive, assertive and take control of the game. A win-win feels good for both sides but always nets less for you. You can make it seem like you're trying to help them with a win-win, but actually have it become more favorable for you.

Like I said earlier in the chapter, the company has spent plenty of time and money choosing you. If the hiring manager doesn't get you on board, *he* looks bad. Always remember that it's in their best interest to successfully hire you.

How to Negotiate Your Offer

- Wait until you get the offer to discuss salary. This will provide you with more leverage since the number of candidates will be smaller and the company will be convinced that you are the perfect candidate.

- Ask for a couple days to consider the offer no matter how excited you are. Express your appreciation but never accept the offer immediately.

- Research to prepare yourself for salary negotiations. Use **Glassdoor.com**, **Payscale.com** and **Salary.com** to figure out the average salaries of people in your field with comparable experience, the city where the company is located, and average salaries for people currently working with the company making you the offer.

- Understand the value of the benefits the company is offering you like health insurance, 401K, bonus, vacation time, etc. Research to find out if they are average and if not, and negotiate these benefits, too. You can request additional paid days off or vacation days, compensation for relocation expenses, etc.

- Rehearse the toughest parts of the negotiation. A mentor could mock negotiate with you.

- Utilize your talents during salary negotiations. If you're a good writer, submit your counter-proposal in writing, while effective speakers can schedule a phone call or meeting.

- Decide on a goal for your salary based on research. Then request to be paid 10-25% higher than that. If the company decides to counter you, it may already be at or higher than your goal. There's also the chance that the company accepts your higher offer.

- If the employer refuses to negotiate your starting salaries, request performance-based bonuses or a signing bonus.

- Constantly remind your new employer the value you bring to the company and how you will help drive results.

- After making a counteroffer, be ready for a number of different responses (including acceptance, rejection, or acceptance with minor compromises).

- If the employer agrees to your requested salary or counteroffer, do not request additional money. This is unprofessional, and the job offer could be dropped.

- Request the accepted offer in writing. If a company refuses to do this, they are being extremely unprofessional, and you need to reconsider your desire to work for them.

- Realize that you do not have to be an expert in negotiation tactics to be successful. Get over any fears you have, understand these negotiation basics and you will do fine.

Things To Avoid

- Do not get emotional. Controlling your emotions is key to success.

- Do not demand a salary that you refuse to budge on. Being professional means being able to compromise.

- Do not continue to negotiate after deciding to accept an offer.

- Do not participate in salary negotiations if you plan on refusing whatever the company offers.

- Do not be pessimistic during salary negotiations. A manager might be able to sense whether you have a poor attitude.

- Do not make ultimatums or leave the negotiating table if you have no other offers.

- Do not make empty threats like "If you don't give me this salary I'm gone."

Personal Challenge
Negotiate to "No" (1 day)

For this challenge I'd like you to find something or someone to negotiate with. It could be a friend, teacher, local shop, online store, or service provider.

I want you to negotiate with that person to get something you want. Once they agree, I want you to negotiate for more...until you hear "no." For example, you could ask a friend for a bite of their sandwich. Then you could ask for another bite. Then you could ask for the entire thing. You should get a "no" somewhere in the process. This challenge will teach you how to get something you want, have the confidence to ask for more and then gracefully accept your rejected request.

The Final Chapter - There Is No Success Without Failure

"Waste your money and you're only out of money, but waste your time and you've lost a part of your life." - *Michael LeBoeuf*

"Success is a lousy teacher. It seduces smart people into thinking they can't lose." – *Bill Gates*

There Is No Success Without Failure

Some day, you find yourself at a low point in your life or your career. A day when you think the world is against you, when other tells you that you're a failure and you begin to believe them. On this day, you have another choice. You can either give up and change course…or renew your faith in yourself and overcome these feelings. The eleven people that I mention below made the second choice, refusing to give up.

Soichiro Honda

Soichiro was turned down by Toyota Motor Corporation for a job after interviewing for a job as an engineer. He was unemployed for an extended period of time and decided to start making scooters of his own at home. His neighbors pushed him to start his own business, and through a series of failures and turns of luck, he built the billion-dollar business that we know today as Honda Motors.

Akio Morita

Morita was distraught when his first product, a rice cooker, sold less than 100 units. He and his business partners saw this failure as an opportunity to improve and continued trying to grow their company, Sony.

Walt Disney
Mr. Disney was fired from an early newspaper job because the editor believed that "he lacked imagination and had no good ideas." After being let go, Disney began a number of businesses that ended with bankruptcy and failure. Still, her persevered and today his company has become a household name, a staple of childhood entertainment and an incredibly lucrative merchandise, movie and theme-park conglomerate.

Albert Einstein
This world-famous theoretical physicist did not speak until he was four years old, and did not read until age seven. Consequently, both his parents and teachers believed him to be mentally handicapped and anti-social. Eventually, he was expelled from school and was denied admittance to the Zurich Polytechnic School. Most would give up, but Einstein took another path, which eventually led to a Nobel Prize and world-renown for his discoveries.

Abraham Lincoln
While today he is remembered as one of the greatest leaders of American history, Lincoln wasn't always so successful. In his younger years he went to war a captain and was demoted to private. His multiple business ventures all met with failure, and this now-legendary political leader was defeated many time when running for public office. Still, he was not deterred from his goals, and his vision for an American nation has shaped the country as it exists today. [1]

Michael Jordan
Today, he is honored as perhaps the best basketball player of all time. In high school, Michael Jordan was actually cut from the school basketball team his junior year. Sheer determination drove Jordan to make the team at UNC, and later for the Chicago Bulls. Late in his career, Jordan stated, "I have missed more than 9,000 shots in my career. I have lost almost 300 games. On 26 occasions I have been

entrusted to take the game winning shot, and I missed. I have failed over and over and over again in my life. And that is why I succeed." [2]

Richard Branson

This billionaire owner of the Virgin empire has embarked on over two-hundred business ventures in his life, many of which were failures. Ventures like Virgin Cola and Virgin credit cards have lost him hundreds of millions of dollars over his lifetime but he never lets occasional failure discourage him from continuous innovation. [2]

J. K. Rowling

Ever heard of Harry Potter? The first book was rejected by twelve publishing houses. A year after Rowling's book met its initial rejections, the eight-year old daughter of Bloomsbury's (publishing house that previously rejected her book) chairman, told her father to publish the book. At the time Rowling was penniless, severely depressed, divorced and trying to raise a child on her own while attending school and writing a novel. Five years later, she had become one of the richest women in the world. [3] To this day, her imaginative, exciting stories have a devoted following of children *and* adults.

Oprah Winfrey

Oprah was fired from her television reporting job because they told her she wasn't fit to be on screen. Ignoring those opinions, she moved on to become the undisputed queen of television talk shows. [4] She has been ranked the richest African-American of the 20th century, the greatest Black philanthropist in American history, and was for a time the world's only Black billionaire. Her worldwide influence has proven that the initial judgment of her 'suitability' for the screen was inaccurate. [5]

Adam Khoo

Khoo was expelled from St Stephen's Primary School at the age of eight for misbehavior, partly due to poor academic results. Back then, Khoo's parents and teachers described him as capable but lazy, indifferent and addicted to television. Yet a five-day program and love of neuro-linguistic programming changed his life. By the age of twenty-six, he was one of the youngest millionaires in Singapore. Now Khoo owns and runs several businesses in education, training, event management and advertising, with a combined annual revenue of over thirty million. This once 'lazy, indifferent' child is certainly motivated now. [6]

Arnold Schwarzenegger
Schwarzenegger came to America in September 1968 at the age of 21, speaking little English. By the age of 30, Schwarzenegger was a millionaire, well before his legendary Hollywood career. A series of successful entrepreneurial ventures and investments gave him financial independence. Later in life, he decided he wanted to run for office. Karl Rove, the Republican mastermind for George W. Bush, mocked his political chances in California. He was the Governor for two terms. Some would consider him the greatest immigrant success story of our time. [7] [8]

The Walking Contradiction

I'm a social engineer, a corporate-trained entrepreneur, a casual reader who writes carefully, and a self-taught teacher. Contradictions, yes. But they also represent perseverance and confidence.

Did I think that my small town upbringing would instill me with a superior sense of openness? That my engineering school would immerse me in a multicultural melting pot? That my first job would give me international business experience? That my second would let me train hundreds of professionals? That I would employ foreign nationals in my first company? Or that my love of teaching would help me to get over my fear of writing and complete this book?

No. The simple truth is that I have always lived my own life, been open to serendipity and believed in myself.

I've had thousands of key choices and forks in the road, each with the potential to lead to vastly different outcomes. With each decision, I solidify my own passions and pursuits, and discover new elements of business, learning and life that I couldn't possibly have foreseen. Eventually, each decision led me to this point: an intersection combining my passions, multicultural experiences, and relationships, with my fields of expertise.

I have failed many times and picked myself back up, ignoring negativity and ridicule. Though some may deem this naiveté, I know that my fortitude has led to my success. My outlook has not only driven me, but allowed me to be happy along the way.

Now you have at your disposal all of the knowledge and skills to succeed. Your last challenge is to train yourself to never give up. Your happiness will not be achieved easily; there is a long, twisting road ahead with thousands of difficult choices to make.

Decide what is important to you and take steps every day to improve. If you do this and believe in yourself, there is only one possible outcome: SUCCESS.

Recommended Reading

As I said, I want you to take as much action as possible...most of which doesn't include reading. Just in case you have some free time after you get your job, though, I'm going to give you a few of my favorite books and websites to help you on your journey.

For additional categories, including entrepreneurship, language learning, etc., be sure to visit our comprehensive companion site.

My Top 3

These three books had a profound impact on my career and I believe they will change you too.

The Four Hour Work Week
By Tim Ferriss

The Medici Effect: What Elephants & Epidemics Can Teach Us About Innovation
By Frans Johansson

The E-Myth Revisited: Why Most Small Businesses Don't Work and What to Do About It
By Michael E. Gerber

Personal Transformation Books

Read this books if you want to build your confidence, become happier and open your mind.

Vagabonding
Rolf Potts

The Art of Happiness
His Holiness the Dalai Lama, Howard C. Cutler

The 48 Laws of Power
By Robert Greene

Other Great Business Books

Read this books if you want to become an entrepreneur.

The Education of Millionaires: Everything You Won't Learn In College About How To Be Successful
By Michael Ellsberg

The 80/20 Principle: The Secret to Success by Achieving More with Less
By Richard Koch

The Magic of Thinking Big
By David J. Schwartz

The Lean Startup
By Eric Ries

Bonus Chapters

This book is not just what you hold in your hands. There was much more but I could not contain all of the information in this book.

How to Start a Company in 7 Days
(includes step-by-step guide)
How to Quit Your Job Without Burning Bridges
(includes real scripts)
The Secret to Career Happiness
(includes case studies)
How to Juggle a Startup and a Full-Time Job
(includes case studies)

For this and much more reader-only content, visit our companion site www.cultureadapt.com.

Acknowledgements

To my loving girlfriend, Asie, who has supported me throughout my entrepreneurial endeavors. Her daily support gave me the courage to finish this book. I see greatness in her and can't wait to help her achieve her dreams as she did with me.

I'd like to thank my parents for their undying support throughout the years. I recognize the struggles they overcame to help me achieve my dreams. Without them I wouldn't be half the man that I am today. I will be forever grateful and someday hope to repay half of what I have been given.

To my mentor, Sharon Wulf, who has been the single greatest influence on my entrepreneurial career. She believed in me before most (including myself) believed I had the potential to do great things. She helps without expecting anything in return and if I am ever half the teacher that she is, I will be ecstatic.

To Suzanne, who trusted an eccentric entrepreneur to do something great. Her charming attitude and mastery of the English language made me sound more eloquent than I could ever actually be. You'll always be an amazing writer, teacher, and look forward to seeing you become an entrepreneurial success yourself.

To Krishna, Amar, Wei, Mihaela, Jnanesh, Eva, and all the other people that allowed me to learn about their amazing life stories. This book would not have been possible without your intelligence and wisdom.

To my sisters, Natalie and Karen, for pushing me throughout my life. For being smarter, more driven and nicer than I. You're better role models than most could hope for.

To all my brothers who would stop a truck if it came in my way. They have mentored me, helped build my confidence, and shaped me throughout my life. They were the catalyst to my own social transformation. They may never know how truly grateful I am for their friendship.

To my first students Meng and Andrew for giving me the confidence to continue pursuing this career. I know you will become successful in whatever you choose and will forever be your friend.

To Lewis Howes who is an amazing teacher and inspired me to take action myself. Who would have known that a single click on a Facebook ad would change my entire life.

To Coach Smith, a mentor throughout my life, that taught me many lessons on the basketball court as well as off. How you trusted 15-year-old me I will never know, but you helped shape my life.

To Rob Moore, a mentor early in my professional career. I learned a lot from you and appreciate the time you spent with me. Still amazed by how parallel our lives have been.

To Michael Cassady, for all the years of friendship, good times and competitiveness. From playing basketball on warm summer days to Budweiser signs, there are more good memories than I write. I look forward to many more ahead.

To all my American and international friends, I'm eternally grateful for all the relationships that I've been able to build with you over the years. The world truly is a remarkable place and I couldn't have imagined my life any differently.

Notes

Chapter 2

[1] - http://www.iie.org

Chapter 5

[1] -
http://www.fourhourworkweek.com/blog/2009/01/20/learning-language/

Chapter 6

[1] - http://www.university-bound.com/facts/youngest-and-oldest-degrees/
[2]- http://www.huffingtonpost.com/2012/07/18/shafay-thobani-8-year-old_n_1684186.html
[3] - http://www.socialtriggers.com

Chapter 8
[1] - Enterprise Systems, 7 Tips for Powerful Networking

Chapter 9
[1] Macionis, John, and Linda Gerber. "Chapter 3 - Culture." Sociology. 7th edition ed. Toronto, ON: Pearson Canada Inc., 2010. 54. Print.
[2] Cross et al., 1989; Isaacs & Benjamin, 1991
[3] http://en.wikipedia.org/wiki/Culture_shock
[4]
http://en.wikipedia.org/wiki/Hofstede's_cultural_dimensions_theory
[5] http://geert-hofstede.com/united-states.html

Chapter 12

[1] http://www.businessinsider.com/body-language-power-poses-2012-11

Chapter 13

[1] http://www.onlinecollege.org/2010/02/16/50-famously-successful-people-who-failed-at-first/
[2] http://getbusylivingblog.com/famous-people-who-found-success-despite-failures/
[3] http://en.wikipedia.org/wiki/J._K._Rowling
[4] http://www.businessinsider.com/26-successful-people-who-failed-at-first-2012-7
[5] http://en.wikipedia.org/wiki/Oprah_Winfrey
[6] http://en.wikipedia.org/wiki/Adam_Khoo
[7] http://en.wikipedia.org/wiki/Arnold_Schwarzenegger
[8]
http://www.usatoday.com/story/life/books/2012/09/30/schwarzenegger-scandal-memoir/1600597/

Disclaimer

This book is presented solely for educational and entertainment purposes. The author and publisher are not offering it as legal, human resources, or other professional services advice. Readers should always consult with a lawyer who specializes in immigration law for assistance and to discuss facts and circumstances specific to their individual cases. While best efforts have been used in preparing this book, the author and publisher make no representations or warranties of any kind and assume no liabilities of any kind with respect to the accuracy or completeness of the contents and specifically disclaim any implied warranties of merchantability or fitness of use for a particular purpose. Neither the author nor the publisher shall be held liable or responsible to any person or entity with respect to any loss or incidental or consequential damages caused, or alleged to have been caused, directly or indirectly, by the information or programs contained herein. No warranty may be created or extended by sales representatives or written sales materials. Every company is different and the advice and strategies contained herein may not be suitable for your situation.